# The Critical
# Legacy of
# Irving Babbitt

Books by George A. Panichas

*Adventure in Consciousness:*
*The Meaning of D. H. Lawrence's Religious Quest (1964)*

*Epicurus (1967)*

*The Reverent Discipline:*
*Essays in Literary Criticism and Culture (1974)*

*The Burden of Vision:*
*Dostoevsky's Spiritual Art (1977)*

*The Courage of Judgment:*
*Essays in Criticism, Culture, and Society (1982)*

*The Critic as Conservator:*
*Essays in Literature, Society, and Culture (1992)*

*Renaissance and Modern Essays:*
*Presented to Vivian de Sola Pinto in Celebration of His Seventieth*
*Birthday (edited, with George R. Hibbard and Allan Rodway) (1966)*

*Mansions of the Spirit:*
*Essays in Literature and Religion (editor) (1967)*

*Promise of Greatness:*
*The War of 1914-1918 (editor) (1968)*

*The Politics of Twentieth-Century Novelists (editor) (1971)*

*The Simone Weil Reader (editor) (1977)*

*Irving Babbitt: Representative Writings (editor) (1981)*

*Irving Babbitt in Our Time (edited, with Claes G. Ryn) (1986)*

Modern Age: *The First Twenty-Five Years. A Selection (editor) (1988)*

*In Continuity: The Last Essays of Austin Warren (editor) (1996)*

Irving Babbitt, 1865-1933

# The Critical Legacy of Irving Babbitt

## An Appreciation

GEORGE A. PANICHAS

ISI Books

Intercollegiate Studies Institute

Wilmington, Delaware

1999

Cataloging-in-Publication Data

Panichas, George Andrew.
The critical legacy of Irving Babbitt: an appreciation / George A.
Panichas. -- 1st ed. --Wilmington, DE: Intercollegiate Studies
Institute, 199p.

p. cm.

Includes bibliographical references and index.
ISBN 1-882926-22-6

1. Babbitt, Irving, 1865-1933. I. Title.

B945.B124  P36  1998   98-73010
191--dc21     CIP

Published in the United States by:
ISI Books
Intercollegiate Studies Institute
P.O. Box 4431
Wilmington, DE  19807-0431
www.isi.org

Manufactured in the United States of America.

To

Austin Warren

1899-1986

*Friend — Encourager — Exemplar*

*Irving Babbitt* fortifies *us: All through the years, he has given me the sense that though I will often be alone, isolated, in time and place, I have ancestors, an apostolic succession. And to take up his books and read a passage, even one taken at random, seems to fortify me and give me courage.*

—Austin Warren

# CONTENTS

# A Prefatory Note

This book is, in essence, an appreciation of the life, work, and thought of the visionary American teacher and critic, Irving Babbitt. It was my friend the late Austin Warren, distinguished literary critic and man of letters, who first introduced me, more than twenty-five years ago, to his mentor's writings. A mutual concern with some of the troubling problems in American higher education prompted Warren to suggest that I read Babbitt's *Literature and the American College* (1908), which eventually led to my reading his other books more systematically. Warren's suggestion proved to be a great blessing, for until then Babbitt had been for me a name either only briefly mentioned or barely recognized, if not openly disdained, in the academy, which in the end says something about the state of literary studies and criticism in our colleges and universities.

From the very beginning I became aware that Babbitt had handed down to us a great legacy of critical thought relating to urgent literary, aesthetic, educational, philosophical, religious, and social-political questions. That Babbitt approached these questions in interconnecting and interdependent contexts, and that he did not isolate or make them marginal, struck me as one of his most valuable bequests. That, too, his writings, and teachings, boldly tackled moral and ethical issues struck me as being equally valuable. His standards of discrimination and courage of judgment, always in evidence, singularly stamped his achievement. More and more I came to see him as our contemporary—one who ventures into the public square to wrestle strenuously with problems of

1

life, literature, and thought. He spoke, in short, to our condition. The essays assembled in this book were written in appreciative response to the challenge of Babbitt's central ideas and concerns.

Now, sixty-five years after his death, what I call the critical legacy of Irving Babbitt mandates even more vigorous attention. As the essays in this book strive to show, this legacy has a worth and relevance that contemporary American civilization desperately needs. Especially at a time in our history when first principles and the "permanent things" have come under increasing attack from the forces of change, Babbitt's critique of American society and culture has even greater validity. My essays variously explore the content of this critique and attempt not only to identify its enduring worth but also to commend its integrity. As I try to show, Babbitt's critical legacy has the power to develop and enhance the virtues of order and proportion in our lives and work.

Babbitt's legacy should remind us that we do not live by bread alone, and that if we have an outer life to manage, we also have an inner life to nurture. To disjoin the two, as Babbitt makes unmistakably clear, invites dissonant consequences for the human community and for the human soul. His writings, exceptionally translucent in style and argument and scope, bring us into contact with paradigms of character and aspiration. They help us to see the world and to understand it as an organic whole. In no way does Babbitt try to portray the world in illusionary terms. For him the world is inescapable reality, which to confront requires earnestness, vigilance, discipline, fortitude. We can neither erase this reality nor transform it into a dreamworld. But we can, Babbitt never stopped insisting, give order and meaning to the world in which we find ourselves and in which the higher will and the sacredness of person are of supreme operative importance. It is this life-principle that impels the essays found here, individually and collectively, even as they call attention to Babbitt's ability to compel us to make every effort to engage the tensive reality of the world from an inherently moral perspective.

The moral dynamic of Babbitt's achievement is at the very center of his critical mission and ethos, and endows his critical legacy with redeeming value. The essays in this book revolve around this dynamic, attempt to illuminate it, and, hopefully, to penetrate its innermost regions. Babbitt, thus, is viewed in his joint office as a teacher and critic who, to the end, gave his witness. What is the place of the ethical life and the moral life in a world of change and doubt? That question occupied Babbitt in word and work; and it is a question that occupies the essays in this book.

Here it should be especially noted that the religious qualities of Babbitt's work are a corollary concern of this book. Babbitt's religious dimension is too often subordinated to or blurred by his humanistic doctrine. This is a matter that I explore here with the purpose of showing that Babbitt was a genuine seeker after religious truths, and that his writings perceive and affirm the synthesizing values of religion both in individual life and in the community. As such his legacy has universal referents. The claim, long and often made, that Babbitt was, in matters of religion, a secularist, a Stoic, a pragmatist, even a denier, is inspected here, and corrected. For Babbitt, Christianity and Aristotelianism, and Buddhism and Confucianism, are convergent paths to the life of moral effort and excellence and of humility.

My appreciations of Babbitt have a generalist as well as an eclectic and reflective stance, and seek to engage the attention of the general reader. The titles of my essays should also signal my critical intentions: to highlight Babbitt's legacy and, in turn, to plead for the restoration and reclamation of its constituent principles.

The essays, as they unfold and interweave, underline what for me are some of the chief features and strengths of the legacy of a teacher and critic whose critical mission deviated neither from its defined goals nor from its centripetal rhythm of judgment. The range of Babbitt's contribution is to be seen in comparative relation to other renowned modern thinkers, both American and European, who with Babbitt combatted the crisis of modernism. In both its comprehensiveness and its universality, his critical legacy has a prophetic thrust that goes beyond geographical boundaries.

Critical recognition of Babbitt's visionary qualities is slowly but steadily growing, as serious studies of his achievement continue to appear. Certainly the scant attention paid to Babbitt twenty-five years ago is now being replaced by increasingly respectful estimations of his worth to us. But we need to have more than simply academic evaluations of Babbitt's writings and ideas, which have an even more compelling meaning as the twentieth century nears a close. It is the uniqueness of Babbitt's critical legacy, its living value and meaning to civilization itself, that now needs to be appreciated by a new generation of readers who have been affected precisely by those conditions that Babbitt saw as shaking the foundations of human existence. Above all, the moral sense, which Babbitt saw as being imperiled at all levels, should receive our most pressing consideration. The erosion of the moral sense is particularly acute in the post-modern world in which nihilist and anarchist tendencies multiply and congeal. In such a world the legacy of Babbitt's ideas can play an influential and reparative role.

It is my hope that this book will spur interest in Babbitt's legacy, and also elicit response to the moral sense, as it transforms into moral responsibility, which he viewed as indispensable to the survival of humane civilization. I want to reiterate that the essays that follow constitute a sympathetic appreciation of what Babbitt has bequeathed to us. I make no claim whatsoever that this book is a systematic analysis of Babbitt's corpus. The use of the word *appreciation* in the subtitle of the book should alert readers to my designated critical aim. If criticism is defined as the judgment of vision, appreciation, even when it must necessarily participate in this process, is gratitude to vision. Here, then, I am pleased to present writings that beckon a reader to share in my appreciation of Babbitt's contribution to American life and letters, and also to join me in grateful recognition of the beneficences of his critical legacy.

## CHAPTER ONE

# Teacher and Critic

## I

Born in Dayton, Ohio, on August 2, 1865, Irving Babbitt was the son of Edwin Dwight and Augusta (Darling) Babbitt. He came of a family founded in America by Edward Bobet, or Bobbett (later spelled Babbitt), an Englishman who settled at Plymouth, Massachusetts, in 1643. In his early years Irving lived in New York City; in East Orange, New Jersey; and in Madisonville, Ohio, where he developed as a country boy after the death of his mother. When his father, a physician, remarried, the family went to live in Cincinnati. Here he attended Woodward High School. He spent two summers working as a reporter in Cincinnati and then a while as a cowboy on an uncle's ranch in Wyoming.

Eventually, with help from relatives, Babbitt came East to enter Harvard College in 1885. Upon graduation with Final Honors in Classics in 1889, he accepted a position at the College of Montana, in Deer Lodge. Then, in 1891-1892, with money he had saved, he went to study in Paris, returning to the Harvard Graduate School, where he met Paul Elmer More (1864-1937), who eventually became his lifelong friend and ally. He took the A.M. degree in 1893, in the autumn becoming an instructor in Romance languages at Williams College. In 1894 he received an appointment at Harvard, where he taught for the rest of his life. He was made a full professor of French literature in 1912, though he taught for the most part in the department of comparative literature.

In London on June 12, 1900, Babbitt married Dora May Drew. Their daughter, Esther, was born in 1901 and their son, Edward Sturges, in 1903. In 1926 he became a corresponding member of the Institute of France, and in 1930 he was elected to the American Academy of Arts and Letters. He was also a fellow of the American Academy of Arts and Sciences. In June 1932 he received the honorary degree of Doctor of Humane Letters from Bowdoin College. Irving Babbitt died in Cambridge, Massachusetts, on July 15, 1933.[*]

These bare facts hardly suggest the depth and intensity of the life of the mind that Babbitt lived. Nor do they capture the excitement surrounding the movement which, under the name of the New Humanism (or Neohumanism), developed in America during the first three decades of the twentieth century, and of which Babbitt was the chief critical theorist and More the most gifted critical practitioner. (Theirs was a transcendent partnership of principles, sustained "by long association and by a fundamental sympathy of mind not incompatible with clashing differences," as More wrote.) If humanism, as it is said, is never new, it must constantly face new problems in any place and in any age. By humanism Babbitt meant the affirmation of man, of man's world of value, and of the faculty in his nature that sets him apart from "a merely quantitative order" and from the chances and changes of time. Babbitt pitted humanism as a third possible attitude toward life against naturalism and supernaturalism, or as he declared, "The problem is to find some middle ground between Procrustes and Proteus."

The New Humanism was a truly conservative

---

[*]For a more detailed examination of the life of Babbitt, see the Appendix to this book, pages 194-206.

humanism that opposed literary avant-gardists, naturalistic psychologists, uncritical traditionalists, liberals, collectivists, progressivists, and pragmatists. The positive and critical humanist, as Babbitt termed him, though he does not disavow the religious life, for "one must insist that religion is the height of man," lives in the secular realm, which he must strive to save from the defects of humanitarianism (for example, the myth of man's natural goodness, the lack of seriousness in the body politic, and indifference to moral principle). In the will to refrain (that is, the need to assert a "veto power" over "the despotism of mood" and an "inner check" upon the expansion of natural impulse, as well as a unifying exercise and expression of "the higher will") he found a mediating point between humanism and religion. Indeed, in Francis Bacon's utilitarianism and in Jean Jacques Rousseau's romanticism Babbitt discerned the undermining not only of the Judaeo-Christian religious tradition but also of the older tradition of humanism, going back to ancient Greece.

The New Humanism attracted many adherents in colleges and universities, especially among teachers of literature. Gradually a voluminous literature regarding it came to be written by adherents and by antagonists. The high point of the critical debate between the two factions occurred in 1930 with the publication of two books, *Humanism and America: Essays on the Outlook of Modern Civilisation,* edited by Norman Foerster, and *The Critique of Humanism: A Symposium,* edited by C. Hartley Grattan. Inevitably the restrictive essences of New Humanism, which George Santayana wrongly associated with the Genteel Tradition of Massachusetts and which H. L. Mencken chose to deride as "gloomy humors," worked against its popular acceptance. Its austerely conservative diagnosis of social and cultural conditions could hardly compete with public demand for social action at a time that found the United States sinking into the Great Depression. John Dewey (1859-1952) was deemed a more appropriate spokesman of national aspirations. His radical optimism concerning the human capacity for reconstructive change and his view of life as a social experience of "shared good" were found more fitting to the national mood. Bread and butter, not "the aristocracy of true distinctions," or the lessons of caution, or the verdict of tradition, were to win the day. What validity has a humanist "communion" of "angry professors," asked Malcolm Cowley,

> for the mill hands of New Bedford and Gastonia, for the beet-toppers of Colorado, for the men who tighten a single screw in the automobiles that march along Mr. Ford's assembly belt? ... And what, in turn, has Humanism to do with the scene outside my window: with the jobless men who saunter in the dusk, or the dying villages, or the paper mill abandoned across the river—this mill whose owners have gone South where labor is cheap?[1]

On occasion equally harsh reaction from even the intellectual right greeted the critical views of the New Humanists, especially as found in "The Fallacy of Humanism," an essay by Allen Tate which appeared in 1929. "[Their] doctrine of restraint does not look to unity," Tate claimed, "but to abstract and external control—not to a solution of the moral problem, but to an attempt to get the moral results of moral unity by main force, by a kind of moral fascism."[2] Tate also argued that the humanists had no method, no unifying living center of action and judgment, no "definite and living religious background." In short, humanism was not enough: "It is an effort to imitate by rote the natural product of culture; it is a mechanical formula for the recovery of civilization." If, then, the values for which the humanists plead are to be realized, "the background of an objective religion, a universal scheme of reference, is necessary." More himself admitted that Tate "has laid hold of some of the real difficulties inherent in the humanist movement as it is now conducted."

Although the reputation of the New Humanism as a doctrine and a movement faltered, its influence, in ideas and ethics, did not. Even the unusual aggressiveness of those attacking Babbitt ("this drill-sergeant," Rebecca West called him) and More (a "banker-conservative," as he was labeled in the *New Republic*) registers the seriousness with which their analysis of American letters and society was taken. Clearly, the New Humanism had a profound educational impact. Walter Jackson Bate, in placing Babbitt's achievement among the major texts of criticism, concludes, "To a degree unsurpassed by any other writer of the last half century, he made traditional critical issues a vivid and living concern, applicable to almost every aspect of modern life."[3] If, too, the New Humanists were dissatisfied with modern literature, prompting even a friendly critic like F. O. Matthiessen to cite their "inadequate sensibility that is a sign of the divorce between mind and experience,"[4] their insistence upon standards of discrimination and taste had a beneficial influence. In this respect Babbitt and More sought to strengthen and dignify the office of the critic in the contexts of selecting, weighing, defining, and "ever checking the enthusiasm of the living by the authority of the dead," as More writes in an important essay, "Criticism." To the critical function they ascribed a higher, sapiential purpose, the Arnoldian belief that a definite end must be kept in view. The critics, More asserted, "stand with the great conservative forces of human nature, having their fame certified by the things that endure amid all the betrayals of time and fashion."[5]

Babbitt never flinched from what he viewed as his commanding office as a teacher and critic. His critical position sanctioned neither retreat nor rerouting. From the start he chose to travel on one road. Like Archilochus's hedgehog, Babbitt knew one big thing, related everything to a central vision, and affirmed a single, universal, organizing principle. He never betrayed his conscience, the truths of which, once he had discovered them, he possessed altogether, avoiding "sudden conversions" and scorning "pistol-shot transformations." His doctrine is characterized not by a program of ambition or even by a rectitude of judgment but by a forthright acceptance of limitation as the law of the manifested world and, consequently, of man's need for self-discipline and self-reliance. Babbitt was to become a lay preacher to Americans whose ministration revolved around conscience rather than grace. His innately Protestant sensibility was to be schooled by his classicist and Orientalist metaphysics in their assimilated forms and consecrated to "the service of a high, impersonal reason." In the end his humanism became a finely wrought reconciliation of East and West, of Confucius and Aristotle, of Buddha and Christ.

Possessing an absolute and undeceived integrity, Babbitt had no pretensions or poses. He discloses the rigorous workings not only of a "conservative mind" but also of a "universal mind," always speaking directly, with courage of judgment and with that tenacity of character associated with the New England mind and conscience. To be regretted, the dark thought will occur to some readers, is the absence of a compassionate mind, a mind that is ever in intimate dialogue with the heart. Words like "sympathy," "love," "charity," "kindness," "pity" are not a visible part of Babbitt's vocabulary. As critical polemicist and check, he refused to "put on sympathy a burden that it cannot bear" and allowed nothing to muddle his censorious inspection of the conditions of existence. The pitiless facts of human experience, he stressed, were incontrovertible. Pointing to similarities between the dilemma of ancient Rome and the dilemma confronting modern America, he warns: "We, too, seem to be reaching the acme of our power and are at the same time discarding the standards of the past. This emancipation has been accompanied by an extraordinary increase in luxury and self-indulgence." To treat the ills of modern civilization Babbitt offered what he himself called an "unamiable suggestion": "The democratic contention that everybody should have a chance is excellent provided it means that everybody is to have a chance to measure up to high standards."

In order to measure Babbitt's contribution as a critic, one must first discern his place as a teacher. For him there was no strict division between two interacting ministries, two interdependent disciplines. Neither can exist without the other, though the quality of the combination must depend on the power of the mind in which the two are combined. A teacher who has no critical viewpoint is no teacher; a critic who ignores or tries to conceal his role as a teacher is no critic. As a teacher Babbitt embraced a doctrine, taught and argued it, reinforced it, sustained it. His teachings, his criticism, are imbued with a finality of belief and decision and constitute a law in tone and temper. It can be safely conjectured that, had he not become a teacher, he would have made an excellent theologian. In both his teaching and his criticism one can hear the voice of the theologian expounding the *logos* of his doctrine. Such a position is not so much to be defended as to be asserted, argued, and affirmed as revealed truth. In the end he gives instruction in the basic doctrines of his catechesis.

Babbitt was no ordinary teacher. He possessed conviction and determination, as well as zest and militancy, seldom seen in the academic world. He made his mark despite the fact that his teachings were intellectually and spiritually incompatible with his time. His influence was as enduring as it was paradigmatic. T. S. Eliot captures its full force when he recalls:

> Yet to have been once a pupil of Babbitt's was to remain always in that position, and to be grateful always for (in my case) a very qualified approval.... If one has once had that relationship with Babbitt, he remains permanently an active influence; his ideas are permanently with one, as a measurement and test of one's own. I cannot imagine anyone coming to react against Babbitt. Even in the convictions one may feel, the views one may hold, that seem to contradict most important convictions of Babbitt's own, one is aware that he himself was largely the cause of them. The magnitude of the debt that some of us owe to him should be more obvious to posterity than to our contemporaries.[6]

Nor was he an ordinary critic. The most impressive characteristic of his criticism is that it contains the voice of a teacher. Its final imprint is its didactic tone, severe, magistrative, uncompromising, urgent—inescapably repetitive, as it must always be in the teaching process. Babbitt's is the style of a teacher ever aware of the dual purpose of nourishing followers and converting enemies. It is a style that is a call to action, a missionary style, for within and beyond the words Babbitt is concerned with the survival of humane civilization.

Education, literature, religion, and politics have a common frontier and constitute the basic area, even the *raison d'être*, of Babbitt's teaching and criticism. "He had given you theses about literature, about life," Stuart P. Sherman writes of his teacher, "which you would spend a lifetime in verifying."[7] In his critical and intellectual pursuits he was, to use an older designation, a generalist, or, to use more modern usage, a comparatist. In his cultural outlook he was an ecumenist, a designation that, at least in his day, was neither honored nor honoring. Bravely and persistently, for there were—and always are—collegial cynics and adversaries to contend with, he refused to see teaching as a one-dimensional task. Teaching was a total process of commitment to creating an ethos and defining a critique. Yet, curiously, he has at times been regarded as a sort of rough-hewn provincial, his worth in the meanwhile underestimated or even derided. "Babbitt, one must conclude," René Wellek writes, "remained an American Republican and a Protestant, however high may have been his regard for the role of the Roman Church, and however far he was from subscribing to any definite Protestant creed."[8]

The reasons for the neglect or the abuse of Babbitt are not difficult to find. The modern age is imperiously scientific and skeptical. To resist this historical fact involves grave risks for a teacher-critic. The risks are apt to be all the more costly when opposition to secular values comes in the form of vigorous protest and argument. At the heart of Babbitt's critique of the main power centers of modern society—utilitarianism, empiricism, positivism, liberalism—is a moral toughness. Against the twentieth-century relativism of the "sociological dreamers and reformers" he set the ancient struggle between good and evil in man rather than in society. This was perhaps his most uncompromising doctrine, as well as the impelling principle of his critique of the Baconian-Rousseauistic point of view.

Babbitt believed that standards have been under attack especially since the eighteenth century, which he identified with Rousseau and with the ascendance of "the temperamental view of life." To obtain general universal standards, then, constitutes an urgent intellectual and spiritual need in a modern world in which relativity and anarchy increasingly supervene. For the critical humanist, having standards is a dual process of selection and rejection and, on the ethical and the aesthetic level, of the "imitation" of a standard. Standards resist the meretricious, the impressionistic, the illusionary, and the merely experimental. They represent what is immutable and transcendent; what is of fixed and permanent worth and yet, as Babbitt unfailingly emphasized, is always tempered by the sense of change and instability. Standards, then, give intrinsic meaning to value, soundness to judgment, and order to vision, are the mediating and unifying formulation of truths that view man in his possibilities and limitations. A bulwark against formlessness, multiplicity, and meaninglessness, they are inevitably centered in a scale of values. "To have standards," he wrote, "means practically to have some principle of unity with which to measure mere manifoldness and change." Babbitt's stress on "analytical intellect," on "power of control," on "poised and proportionate living" was largely derived and sustained by this principle.

The deterioration of the ethical and moral life he saw as a concomitant of the loss of the classical spirit and the resultant "pursuit of strangeness and adventure." Babbitt was protesting against a Benthamite, "causo-mechanical" world in which the life of value receded before the philosophy of change. His affirmation of the life of value is tied to the requirement of vital control, which signifies an acceptance of discipline that embodies the presence and application of standards, leads to an avoidance of excess, and recognizes an ethical "self" that is capable of exercising control and a natural "self" that needs controlling. Babbitt was an absolutist who believed in making a distinction between moral progress and material progress, between the spirit of permanence and the law of change, between reverence for "the limit" and romantic longing for the infinite. At the center of all distinctions, he placed the eternal opposition of the qualitative and the quantitative views of life. In embracing the latter, he contended, lay the beginning of error, of which a growing absorption in the present, an emphasis on specialization, and a neglect of tradition and of anything related to an identifiable center of values were some of the more alarming manifestations.

In his teaching and criticism Babbitt was continuously exercising a dialectic. His allegiance to it was undeviating, as he connected it with first principles, on which, he claimed, the modern world had gone wrong. Reverence, discipline, wisdom, proportion, decorum, standards: these composed the formative terms of his dialectic. In the best sense, he used a language that belonged to a classical tradition, to the wisdom of the ages, as he liked to put it. Doubtlessly, the Great War of 1914-1918 did much to diminish the authority and integrity of such a language. But the fault, Babbitt claimed, did not lie in the credibility of language itself, which he equated with what is universal and human, but with its corruptive conversion into what is local and relative. Cultural breakdown had progressed with the indiscriminating liberalism of an age in which man entered a Rousseauistic dreamland; in which, symptomatically, "the great illusion is not war but humanitarianism." "The results of the material success and spiritual failure of the modern movement are before us. It is becoming obvious to everyone that the power of Occidental man has run very much ahead of his wisdom."

Babbitt adhered to the old struggle between good and evil within man: "The true dualism I take to be the contrast between two wills, one of which is felt as vital impulse (*élan vital*) and the other as vital control (*frein vital*)." In this dualism he recognized an enduring element within man that sets him apart from the everlasting flux, that accentuates a sense of values, and that gives man a purposive character. The acceptance of the dualistic philosophy was for Babbitt a criterion of truth and value. He was no less critical of "pantheistic dreamers" who have sought to substitute "the grace of nature" for "the grace of God," since this substitution discloses the absence of the will to refrain that leads to spiritual anarchy and "endless self-deception." In the political realm, too, Babbitt saw the requirement of the dualistic element. The constitutional democrat's drive for institutions that act as checks on the immediate will of the people, he believed, is an instance of the principle of control. He goes on to say: "The partisan of unlimited democracy on the other hand is an idealist in the sense the term assumed in connection with the so-called romantic movement. His faith in the people is closely related to the doctrine of natural goodness proclaimed by the sentimentalists of the eighteenth century."

For the recovery of the truth of dualism, Babbitt insisted, modern man must begin by exalting the ethical, or higher, will to the first place: "To give the first place to the higher will is another way of declaring that life is an act of faith." The affirmation of this quality of will he saw as a humanistic rather than as a purely religious act of restraint identifying man as a responsible moral agent. Man's "free temperamental overflow" must be subject to a veto power, to an inner human check. Babbitt associated the higher and active will with the discriminating process of selection and discipline and with the attainment of "the virtues of concentration." This will, as a form of human aspiration, culminates in "a law of the spirit" and in "the law of measure." It aids man's power to harmonize in himself opposite qualities and to disclose and vindicate his humanity, his higher self. Mediating between unity and diversity, between the absolute and the relative, between the One and the Many, it never forgoes the discipline of a central standard that bars a radical pragmatism and constrains an excessive pluralism and monism.

In the modern era of expansiveness, an offshoot of scientific naturalism and the romantic mentality, Babbitt viewed with unease the growing emancipation of the senses, volition, intellect, and conscience. Man's expansive desires become one-sided, disproportionate, overpredominant in his drive, at once self-assertive and self-indulgent, for sheer gratification, spontaneity, intensity—for what Brunetière terms the "morbid and monstrous development of the me." This drive, violating the law of concentration, that special law of unity, measure, and purpose that establishes "a causal sequence between the facts of human nature," as Babbitt expresses it, not only is emotional but also becomes imperialistic as it invades other areas of life and affects scientific, national, political, and commercial tempers, and forces, of expansion. "As against the expansionists of every kind," he declares, "I do not hesitate to affirm that which is specifically human in man and ultimately divine is a certain quality of will, a will that is felt in its relation to his ordinary self as a will to refrain." No words communicate better his identification of the old dualism and the higher will with the old morality in rejecting what More once spoke of as the "New Morality of drifting."

## II

In particular Babbitt views this drift in naturalism, which denies the conflict between man's ethical and natural self, "the civil war in the cave," by insisting that man is merely a part of nature and that man's religious, ethical, and aesthetic values, as they comprise and define the wisdom and the experience of the race, are utterly subordinate to the reality, if not the dogma, of constant flux and relativity. Babbitt believes that the scientific and utilitarian naturalism, started by Bacon, achieves its logical continuation in the sentimental and romantic naturalism of Rousseau, who claimed that for him there was "no intermediary term between everything and nothing." Their fusion revolves around natural law as it absorbs human life in quantitative and dynamic terms. The truth of man's inner life, as reflected in human conduct and character, is geared to the "peripheral enrichment of life" and "training for science and training for power." The alliance of the Baconian idea of progress and the Rousseauistic idea of liberty helped, then, to overthrow humanism. The consequences of the naturalistic conception of life are far-reaching and disastrous. Its most serious consequence is that of diminishing the idea of a law for human nature as being distinct from the laws of the physical world, or as Babbitt states, "Anyone who thus identifies man with phenomenal nature, whether scientifically or sentimentally, is almost inevitably led to value only the virtues of expansion, for according to natural law, to grow is to expand."

Babbitt's oeuvre is a plea for the place of moral effort in human life as a guard against the extremes, as well as the excrescences, of naturalism, of subjective individualism, of materialism, of idealism. This effort is closely connected with analysis and discrimination and with the inner life and the principle of control. It is, for Babbitt, at the very top of the scale of human values. If the vagaries of the expressionistic or the impressionistic are not to lead to a chaos of values, the critical pursuit must have moral roots. "The values of literature, the standards by which it must be criticised, and the scheme according to which it must be arranged, are in the last resort moral." So writes John Middleton Murry in a review of *Rousseau and Romanticism* (1919).[9] His words pinpoint one of the basic purposes, and values, of Babbitt's contribution.

Yet one must approach this dimension of Babbitt's critical thinking cautiously. That is, his stress falls on ethical rather than on metaphysical essences and is rooted in human experience. Though his meaning has appurtenant religious values, insofar as Babbitt posits his critique of modern life on unchanging standards, which must revolve around what he termed a "precise tracing of cause and effect," it is in the end not theologically oriented. Babbitt affirmed a perspective inseparable from the kind of religious empiricism for which he admired Buddha. Such a perspective, containing a "path," he conceived of as leading to a "higher will," revealed in the act of concentration. Specifically human and ultimately religious, it disposed one to acts of a "spiritual strenuousness," which Babbitt called the chief virtue of Buddhism.

His admiration of Christian tradition, with its implicit vision of order and continuity, did not at the same time soften his distrust of its doctrine of salvation, attended as it can be by enticing forms of procrastination. (Babbitt much preferred "a rest that comes through striving.") Hence he was especially sensitive to any shifting of standards, whether the shifting originated with a romanticizing and emotional religionism or with an insidious utilitarianism. The moral process was for Babbitt one of self-restraint, which meant the simultaneous need to resist metaphysical illusion, a rarefying but corruptive form of the tendencies of human expansiveness. In holding to his concepts, Babbitt sought to support the case of a true spirituality. At the core of this discipline he placed a highly concentrated humanism which he himself both qualifies and clarifies when he declares: "I am concerned...less with the meditation in which true religion always culminates, than in the mediation or observance of the law of measure that should govern man in his secular relations."

This concern was critical rather than metaphysical. "Why do you keep wishing me to be a theologian?" he asks one of his followers. "I am merely a critic." For him the moral spirit and the critical spirit are symbiotic. The growth and the refinement of one depends on and informs the other. The critical act is a judgmental act with implications of a prescriptive character. It enables participation in human life, which Babbitt differentiated from the religious experience that he respected but that he saw as potentially static. The critic must create standards in opposition to what is relativistic. He must affirm limits that are moral in their significance. Since there is a law for man and a law for thing, the critic continually makes distinctions and emphasizes the need "for the sharply drawn line of demarcation, for the firm and fast distinction." He constantly engages in "the application of standards of judgment" and searches for *la vraie vérité*. The critical process is inherently moral in its demands and conditions. As Babbitt states, "The greater a man's moral seriousness, the more he will be concerned with doing rather than dreaming (and I include right meditation among the forms of doing)."

Critical judgment epitomizes the capacity for distinction. Babbitt saw it as a basic feature of the humanistic idea of discipline, as an act of choice that translates into the highest critical function, reinforcing the principle of restriction and selection implicit in a standard. Critical judgment also serves as a refining process of concentration, which he believed to be operable or inoperable according to the way in which vital impulse is submitted to vital control. Babbitt was not a casuist. His approach was direct and concrete, rational and never problematic; and his precepts were clear-cut. In delineating his valuations—valuation being one of his most enduring critical preoccupations—he was compelled by conscience. The main task, he asserted, was to avoid, or at least to mitigate, confusions and false analyses and syntheses. Babbitt's position, in keeping with his set of principles, was inherently combative. The issues that he attacked stemmed from the modern tendency, fast becoming a habit, to compromise moral value by glorifying the "new" values of doubt, questioning, relativism—those qualities that culminate in paradox and ambivalence and that dull the line between man and nature.

The imperative of moral discipline is antecedent to the continuity of moral order. It acts as a defense against the expansive tendencies that Babbitt associated with the decay of cultural standards: "Every doctrine of genuine worth is disciplinary and men in the mass do not desire discipline." Without the "disciplinary virtues" no person, and certainly no civilization, can participate in the universal life or be liberated from nonessentials. "Civilization is something that must be deliberately willed; it is not something that gushes up spontaneously from the depths of the unconscious." Humanistic discipline, as it creates and establishes standards of order, is protection against the Bergsonian apostles of flux and evolution, the "votaries of the god Whirl" and of "a universal relativity."

In its critical context Babbitt's world view is inclusive, particularly as this inclusiveness is revealed in his valuations of literature and of the theory of literature as well. His critical theory and practice never deviated from his perception of right order as the source of moral feeling. This line of his critical thought is classical and conservative in its basic premises and formulations and canonic and cosmopolitan in spirit. There is some truth to the charge that Babbitt's work bears the mark of a heresy hunt. Tough and zealous, he was clear about the war that he was fighting and the enemy he was facing. His treatment of intellectual and moral problems was invariably in a state of vigorous, even fierce, reaction, which must maintain active, steady opposition to ideologues who refuse to see the duality of human experience and who subordinate all standards to the doctrine of flux and relativity. "I would react in the name of the modern spirit," Babbitt asserts, in qualifying the forms and the relevance of his own reaction as a "modern of moderns." "For the modern spirit does not necessarily coincide with the naturalistic spirit; it is simply the positive and critical spirit, the spirit that refuses to submit tamely to authority, but would try out and test everything according to the facts."

He was particularly alert to any movement that leads to the obfuscation of the sharp judgment and to the encouragement of sophistry. Though Rousseau marks the beginning of the modern "naturalistic imbroglio," Babbitt saw other enemy faces. Never one to hide behind an academic mask, he confronted his enemy with zealousness and honesty, without a shadow of deflection:

> The critics have lost traditional standards and have failed as yet to find inner standards to take their place; they have, in short, become impressionists. Those critical impressionists are…closely related to philosophers like James and Bergson who reveal in the infinite otherness of things, the warm immediacy of individual impulse, and dismiss everything that makes for unity as cold, inert, merely conceptual.

> The scientist who tries to stretch his observation of natural law to cover the whole of human nature is really being drawn away from the positive and critical attitude into some phantasmagoria of the intellect.… What the present situation would seem to require is not the transcendentalist, but the spiritual positivist who will plant himself on the facts of the human law as firmly as the true scientist does on the facts of the natural law, and who would look with equal disdain on the apriorist and the metaphysician.

One finds in these statements an unhesitating power that invests Babbitt's critical thought with a clarity that is commensurate with moral instruction. He combined the tasks of a diagnostician with those of a pathologist discoursing on the nature and causes of the diseases of modernism. His main function was that of delineating his perception of human dualism. His devotion to this function permanently informed his approach. In it one discovers the value-creating principle of unity that Babbitt adhered to in his critical theory and that undergirds his achievement with the same sureness of purpose that he sees as being at the core of *The Masters of Modern French Criticism* (1912): "My whole volume is meant as a protest against the romantic tendency to withdraw into the tower of ivory—in other words, to treat art and literature as something apart from life." He never deviated from this principle of unity, from this criterion, which, if the critic is to have any responsible standards—if he is to be a critic at all—signifies the attainment of the truths of dualism. Babbitt's moral sense is ancillary to a criticism which "can only come from a progressive knowledge of the inner check."

"If art is to be humanized," Babbitt says, "it must not simply flow with nature but be checked and tempered by some perception of the One." The critic must be vigilant against what Babbitt considered a paramount cause of the fall of cultural standards: anarchy of the emotions and of the imagination. In this respect he was in the vanguard of critical theorists refusing to separate a literary situation from a cultural situation. "Thus to study English with reference to its intellectual content," he writes, "will do more than anything to make it a serious cultural discipline." Babbitt's literary standards interknit with his cultural standards. "The best type of critic may therefore be said to be creative in the sense that he creates standards. It is in their common allegiance to standards that critic and creator really come together." Babbitt's emphasis on classical and religious tradition is in keeping with his task as a conservator. To those living in an age of expansion, the catechistical nature of his critical expression was no doubt exasperating. A critic counseling mediation between appreciation and judgment, let alone repeatedly emphasizing the need for retrenchment, individual and national, could hardly expect a receptive audience. The call to discipline and the affirmation of standards of taste are hardly tolerable in an increasingly pluralistic age in which "creative spontaneity" becomes gospel.

His doctrine of the New Humanism sought to moderate the worst, and the easiest, habits of modern man, or what Babbitt terms "the expansive lusts of the natural man." But his penchant for words like "mediation" and "moderation" was perhaps an unconscious disciplining of his own innermost feeling, and anger. Mediation and moderation were rational antidotes to conditions that struck him as "nothing less than pernicious." But it was for the eradication of these conditions that, intuitively, he worked. That his enemies detected his motives accounts for their fulminations, crystallized in Edmund Wilson's denunciation of Babbitt for conveying opinions which are "the mere unexamined prejudice of a bigoted Puritan heritage...[which he] never succeeded in sloughing off." Babbitt's theory and practice of criticism can be likened to "spiritual exercises," the demanding asceticism of which dictates attitudes of discipline and emphasizes the universality of duty. But asceticism, whether spiritual or intellectual, has never been one of the goals of modernism, and even the most sensitive critics have chosen to err on the side of naturalism rather than of asceticism. Babbitt recognized precisely this clinging to naturalistic postulates in the ideas of his student Walter Lippmann; and when, in the *Forum*, he reviewed the latter's *A Preface to Morals* (1929), he singled out "the modernist's dilemma" of which this book was a sign: "The modernist has achieved the emancipation from the traditional faith for which he has been striving and is disillusioned regarding the results of his own rebellion."

Moral criteria inform Babbitt's critical theory and practice. These criteria, the guide and impulse to his criticism, revolve around moral effort. (Babbitt unqualifiedly endorses Buddha's words: "Self is the lord of self. Who else can be the lord?...You yourself must make the effort.") Babbitt opposes "the moral real" to "the moral ideal," which he identifies with "anarchy of the imagination": with moral indolence, whether in the form of the romantic confusion of values or of the failure, either as evasiveness or escapism, to exercise restraint. He finds the ideal of romantic morality summarized in Lord Byron's words (from "The Island"): "The wish—which ages have not yet subdued / In man—to have no master save his mood." An aesthetic morality that lacks a universal and ethical quality leads to anarchical attitudes and, hence, to an art of shifting illusions. In the realm of the imagination, Babbitt believes the inner check acts as a moral law against an unbounded aesthetic temperament. Man's moral sense reveals and refines itself in art as a perception of the struggle between good and evil in the individual. This perception is Babbitt's fundamental moral criterion, which in effect announces that the artist attains breadth "not by throwing off but by taking on limitations, and what he limits is above all his imagination." The imagination is an important part of the burden of moral responsibility insofar as it resists the utilitarian and sentimental tendencies of naturalist ethics and also searches for distinctions and definitions. From the tensive interplay of this resistance and this search, Babbitt is saying, arise the standards of "an art of clear and firm outlines."

Whatever the weaknesses or the irritations of his critical methods, it is clear that one is in contact with a powerful and distinguished mind in complete possession of its purpose and pursuing it with firmness and wholesome clearness. Not unlike the Matthew Arnold who, as Babbitt was to write, was misunderstood by his contemporaries not because he was less but because he was more modern than they, Babbitt made judgments out of his relentless concern with the menace of moral and cultural anarchy. His criticism is a censure of art that, lacking the principles of selection, results in the triumph of formlessness over form and of diffuseness over concentration. The good critic must be watchful of two rhythms, the naturalistic and the romantic, that is to say, of two influences and effects, in modern art: "decadent aestheticism" and the "emancipation of the imagination from any allegiance to standards, from any central control." The criteria that Babbitt employs in his judgment of art are those that he honors in Arnold.

## III

The failure to penetrate the moral qualities of Babbitt's criticism has long led to a misunderstanding of his work. Thus, though a perceptive scrutiny of Babbitt's criticism, R. P. Blackmur's essay "Humanism and Symbolic Imagination" fails precisely because, in adhering to what Brooks Adams called "the comfortable muddle," it cannot grasp the moral essences and exigencies of Babbitt's criticism. Blackmur's argument is that the tragedy of Babbitt was his isolation, "the utter desolateness of the center"; that Babbitt was unable to deal with the symbolic imagination without reducing it to an intellectual level:

> He never saw afresh in the imaginative field. He never...attempted to revive the turbulence of the flesh—the fury and the mire, to use Yeats's phrase, in human veins.... He never realized that we inherit only in the flesh, that the spirit is nothing without the letter. He knew nothing, in short, or at any rate never took account of the chthonic underside of things which the topside only keeps down. His interest...lay almost entirely in what could be made to seem exemplary within the

terms of a formula. [10]

Blackmur's essay underlines what is symptomatic of so much modern criticism, even as it points to those habits that Babbitt tirelessly inveighed against. His critical valuations, far from having the disability that Blackmur believes they have, are stringent and in their ethical aim free from any confusion—the outgrowth of an active critical intelligence whose mission is to mobilize the moral sensibility.

Babbitt's aesthetic valuations ultimately emerge, taking their critical shape from his indictment of a romantic imagination that fails to distinguish between the fictitious and the real worlds and perpetuates vision at the expense of discipline. It is an imagination that lingers in the primitivistic, the idyllic, the passional, the illusionary, and ends in retreat into a "land of chimeras," into "an endless and aimless vagabondage of the emotions with the imagination as their free accomplice." Adventure and spontaneity, dreamland and reverie are constituents of this imagination. The real gives way to the ideal, obligations and constraints to fantasy, to sentiment, to nostalgia as "the pursuit of pure illusion." Distinctions separating the different literary genres and also the different arts deteriorate. The romantic, or eccentric, imagination has no center and fails, Babbitt writes, "to disengage the real from the welter of the actual and so achieve something that strikes one still as nature but a selected and ennobled nature." Such an imagination, absolved of restraints or limits, wars against two great traditions and the sustaining ethos of each: against both classical decorum and Christian humility.

Aesthetic romanticism was equated by Babbitt with the evasion of moral responsibility. It points to the victory of shifting illusion over an art of clear and firm outlines as unity of insight becomes unity of instinct. Babbitt insists on the need to deal with both art and life from an ethical center. Art discloses "the high seriousness of the ethical imagination"; it cannot absolve itself from universal values and from common intellectual and moral judgments. The artist can neither ignore nor reject those traditional forms that comprise "the funded experience of any particular community." When he does, the result is one of disconnection. Babbitt shares Edmund Burke's belief that individualism should be humanistic and religious rather than, as Rousseau argued, naturalistic. "If the individual," writes Babbitt, "condemns the general sense, and trusts unduly his private self, he will have no model; and a man's first need is to look up to a sound model and imitate it." With Burke, he believed that much of the wisdom of life consists in the imaginative re-creation of past experience in such a way as to bring it into connection with the present: "The very model that one looks up to and imitates is an imaginative creation." If Rousseau emboldens the imagination of wonder, Burke emboldens the imagination of reverence. The latter imagination is drawn back to an ethical center and supplies a standard "with reference to which the individual may set bounds to the lawless expansion of his natural self (which includes his intellect as well as his emotions)."

The artist, if he is to proffer a humanistic value of wisdom, according to Babbitt, must strive to mediate between the intuition of the Many, when dealing with the natural order, and the intuition of the One, when dealing with man's peculiar domain. Only then does the artist recognize the potentiality in man of a spontaneousness that resists the flux and yet also imposes upon it a human purpose and satisfies a higher standard: "Unless there is something that abides in the midst of change and serves to measure it, it is obvious that there can be no standards." There is, then, an imagination that gives access to the supersensuous and becomes an organ of insight and an imagination that does not rise above sense impressions.

In the philosophy and aesthetic theory of Benedetto Croce (1866-1952), though, Babbitt found some merits—for instance, Croce's indictment of intellectual anarchy, of unbridled individualism, of scientific intellectualism—he also found a central wrongness and void: "In general, nothing could be more romantic than Croce's cult of intuition in the sense of pure spontaneity and untrammelled expression, his tendency to reduce art to a sort of lyrical overflow that is not disciplined to any permanent centre of judgment in either creator or critic and the consequent identification of genius and taste." Croce, said Babbitt, failed to see the One in the Many; denied the validity of genres in literature and art; rejected the Aristotelian view of poetry as a creative imitation of the universal in favor of a view of poetry as expression and lyrical spontaneity. Above all, he found lacking in Crocean aesthetics an effective counterpoise to the expansionist desires, "to the love, namely, of change and motion for their own sake, to the psychic restlessness that is the inner equivalent of the unparalleled increase of power and speed in the outer world."

Following Aristotle, Babbitt taught that centrality of vision is necessary if the creative imagination is to be able to separate unity and purpose from the welter of the actual. Man's craving for the marvelous is, to be sure, necessary, but it must not sacrifice truth to the universal. Coleridge's *The Rime of the Ancient Mariner*, for example, represented for Babbitt the sacrifice of the verisimilar to the marvelous, radically removed from the Aristotelian high seriousness requiring relevancy to normal experience and a relevancy tested in terms of action. Coleridge's poem lacks, he goes on to emphasize, a serious ethical purport and an adequate concern with moral choices as they bear on the problem that finally counts, "that of man's happiness or misery." Imagination that fails to cooperate with reason in the service of the higher self can scarcely create values that have a human significance. In the artist's tendency to exalt the differences between man and man and to denigrate the identities Babbitt detected a confusion between individuality and personality, the latter being something that man must consciously win with reference to a disciplining and humanizing standard set above his temperamental self. In viewing in the literary cults of his time what he regarded as the increasing surrender of discrimination, of control, of human substance to pure spontaneity, Babbitt viewed what he believed to be a drift towards unintelligibility. His prediction, first made in the thirties, has been amply proved: "If we are to judge by *surréalisme* and other recent literary cults the time is approaching when each writer will, in the name of his genius conceived as self-expression, retire so completely into his own private dream that communication will become impossible."

Life gives, and, indeed, man himself is, Babbitt notes, a "oneness that is always changing." Oneness and change are inseparable, a fact which means "that such reality as man can know positively is inextricably mixed up with illusion." If life is but a web of illusions, "a dream within a dream," there is, Babbitt demurs, at the center of all change a unity, as also there are "standards with reference to which the dream of life may be rightly managed only through a veil of illusion." The problem of the One and the Many can be solved only by the right use of illusion, that illusion which, in Joubert's phrase, "is an integral part of reality" and which, if left out of human experience, prompts one to "see the fact or 'law' in hard isolation and not in its mysterious interconnection with the whole." Deeper insight into the role of the imagination can lead to a perception of an abiding unity and provide an organ of insight that achieves "the illusion of higher reality," remaining true to the idea of the universal, that is, something that has purpose, or constraint and effort.

There is a right use of illusion, but there is also a

wrong use when man hungers for sensual or metaphysical illusions—for instance, the glamour of an earthly paradise or the ecstasy of a "false finality." This wrong use Babbitt connects with "reverie," the intense and prolonged enjoyment of a physical impulse and the yearning to live subjectively in an element of fiction that absolves one from "the real labor of thinking" and glorifies half-truths. The indiscriminating use of illusion is still another form of an expansionist tendency. Babbitt tied the element of illusion, in the framework of the play of the imagination, to an essential question that is to be asked of all men: whether one regards liberty as "a taking on or as a throwing off of limitations." Again echoing Aristotle, Babbitt observes, "One may be rightly imitative…and so have access to a superior truth and give access to it only by being a master of illusion."

The mystery of the creative process, of those dimensions of art which are gratuitous and autotelic and manifest creativity as a "magic synthesis," hardly impressed Babbitt. He viewed as unsound the free and virtuosic aspects of art (arising from high spirits, the gratuitous instinct of play, the need for beauty and delight and fantasy, the irresponsible spirit of comedy, of fervor, of mischief). Not the "passion for origins" in creativity and in the study of literature but rather a preoccupation with ends comprised his critical orientation. This concern also marked the intense moral character of Babbitt's critical sensibility. What his antagonists have taken to be his deficiency of aesthetic understanding, he took to be the core and strength of his critical ideas: unswerving commitment to the moral consciousness, to which literature as a criticism of life must address itself. Bravely and with perseverance, he pronounced those criteria of literary culture, always in close relation to the social-political situation, that neither in his time nor in ours make popular the critic as moralist. To disabuse one of one's illusions, to break into, tamper with,

and overturn one's dreamland, as Babbitt did with fero-
cious diagnostic power, became a denounceable breach, a
violation, a violence, which others do not easily condone
or forget, and from which they do not easily recover. To
judge by the interminable hostility to Babbitt it is not at all
hard to conclude that he penetrated into areas of life and
thought too vulnerable to tolerate intervention—the vul-
nerability all too often symptomatic of both individual and
national infirmity.

Babbitt never ceased to state the case for criticism. Nor
did he ever relent in affirming the active interdependence
of, if not the parity between, the creative and the critical
states of mind. He refused to accept or to tolerate the aesthetic contention that, as it has been representatively and
exuberantly stated, "the work of art assumes the existence
of the perfect spectator, and is indifferent to the fact that
no such person exists. It does not allow for our ignorance
and it does not cater to our knowledge." He dismissed such
an aesthetic response as a surrender to unchecked expansiveness, to romantic and emotional aestheticism, to "a
rampant naturalism." "Man will always crave a view of life
to which perception lends immediacy and the imaginative
infinitude," Babbitt was to remark of a desire that he found
wanting in discrimination and wisdom. The imagination,
he believed, reaches out, seizes likenesses, and helps to
establish certain constant factors in human experience.
"The obvious reply to those who call for more creation and
less criticism," he writes, "is that one needs to be critical
above all in examining what now passes for creation."

For the critic the act of selection constitutes a constant
process, which Babbitt saw as a counterpoise to excess of
the sympathetic and appreciative temper and to what he
labeled "the romantic confusion of the arts." "What we see
in America to-day, for instance, is an endless procession of
bad or mediocre books, each one saluted on its way to
oblivion by epithets that would be deserved only by a mas-

terpiece," he writes in 1912, his words even more applicable to present circumstances that continue to underline "an undue tolerance for indeterminate enthusiasms and vapid emotionalism." Art and literature that pass from the domain of action into that of reverie exhibit the pursuit of illusion for its own sake and the victory of the senses over intellect, character, and will. In art and literature one must look for strict causal connections and seek to maintain a balance between the analytic and the synthetic elements of one's thought.

How can the creator be saved from "the romanticism of nympholeptic longing" and from "the insurrection from below"? This was a question that Babbitt never ceased to ask—and to answer: "If the arts lack dignity, centrality, repose, it is because the men of the present have no centre, no sense of anything fixed or permanent either within or without themselves, that they may oppose to the flux of phenomena and the torrent of impressions." What he attacked was an imagination set free "to wander wild in its own empire of chimeras": "To assert that the creativeness of the imagination is incompatible with centrality or, what amounts to the same thing, with purpose, is to assert that the creativeness of the imagination is incompatible with reality or at least such reality as man may attain." The creative imagination cannot be excused for defying boundaries and spurning definition: "Both the imagination and the emotion that enter into the romantic symbol are undisciplined.... Great literature is an imaginative and symbolical interpretation of an infinite that is accessible only to those who possess in some degree the same imagination."

The distinction between the two main types, or qualities, of imagination was a distinction between what Babbitt termed an ethical, or permanent, type, which gives high seriousness to creative writing, and an Arcadian, or dalliant, type, which fails to rise above the recreative level.

The latter type, which he viewed as a religion of art, represents a sham religion. It is an imagination in which illusion is not disciplined to the higher reality and which leads to a confusion of values and to "anarchy of the imagination." Sound imagination no less than sound individualism must look to a center and a model and grasp the abiding human element: "A knowledge of it results from experience—experience vivified by the imagination." Man tends to be immersed in his personal conceit and in the kind of illusion peculiar to his time, though there is always, Babbitt notes, the question of degree: "Man realizes that immensity of being of which Joubert speaks only in so far as he ceases to be the thrall of his own ego. This human breadth he achieves not by throwing off but by taking on limitations, and what he limits is above all his imagination."

## IV

It is the critic's responsibility to uphold the idea of value and to defend its viability in an age of doubt. Babbitt recognized both the immediate and the extensive nature of this responsibility in terms of the aristocratic principle of standards that must be established. His perhaps most preeminent standard relates to the critic's mission, of which the controlling goal is that of making moral sense of things. An understanding of Babbitt's criticism must be looked for in this fundamental aspect of his mission. That he refused to exempt literature from moral categories: this pivotal principle empowers his critical thought. It is its propelling constituent, its final measure, and its signifying authority. For Babbitt criticism requires expending a mental effort of precise analysis, which kindles into spiritual insight and refers human experience to a moral center: "Experience after all has other uses than to supply furnishings for the tower of ivory; it should control the judgment and guide the will; it is in short the necessary basis of conduct." Babbitt upheld and illustrated two catechistical truths: that without character there is no intelligence and that without honesty there is no clarity.

Put simply, his mission was that of a critic expounding the humanistic values of "moderation, common sense, and common decency." He saw his mission as imposing on him a destiny, a work of life, as it were. The intrinsic requirement of this mission was unconditional, particularly if discipline and standards were to attain any viable place in cultural life. "One should not be," he cries, "moderate in dealing with error," words that portend the form and scope of his mission. Babbitt himself was aware of the rearguard action he was fighting, if one is to judge by his *Democracy and Leadership* (1924), which can be read as a valedictory statement that has yet to find its audience. Here his message is simple and cogent: the crisis of civilization is inseparable from the crisis of spirit in the modern world. The main source of this crisis is the denial of the dualism of spirit and nature. And the main and most frightening consequence is that, morally and intellectually, the spirit of indolence and conceit spreads through all parts of the body politic. Evil is its most destructive agent. Civilization, as a striving for right order and a way to the hierarchy of values, is its most vulnerable object.

Babbitt rejected dogmatic and revealed religion, as well as ecclesiastical authority and forms of worship. "What you get in the churches nowadays," he said, "is religiosity, the religion of feeling, aestheticism, the cult of nature, official optimism, talk about progress, humanitarian sympathy for the poor." Though he attacked religious obscurantism and enthusiasm, he had strong intellectual respect for orthodox religion, particularly Roman Catholicism, that maintained clearly defined beliefs and civilized standards.

The humanist, he said, "does not seek to define God and is chary of ultimates." But he also admitted that humanism "gains immensely when it has a background of religious insight." A balanced religious sympathy braces Babbitt's critical mission, and repeatedly he pleads for uniting humanistic and religious values. His critical idiom, even when cursorily surveyed, is replete with religious essences, although his use of religious language never becomes opportunistic. He is careful, for example, to point to the romantic corruption of the idea of the infinite: "No distinction is more important than that between the man who feels the divine discontent of religion, and the man who is suffering from mere romantic restlessness." In a large sense Babbitt belongs to "the old criticism," which is tied to the old definitions and categories, to criticism that participates in a moral vision and that proceeds "in multiplying sharp distinctions, and...then put[s] these distinctions into the service of the character and will."

He practiced a religious criticism, though he himself was not a religious critic. "But it is always the human reason, not the revelation of the supernatural, upon which Mr. Babbitt insists," Eliot wrote in 1927.[11] Babbitt revealed, at its best, the cooperation between the critical and the religious spirit. He nevertheless stressed that criticism must respond to the "immediate data of consciousness," that the significance of human life must develop from a religious empiricism: "No inconsiderable part of wisdom consists in just this: not to allow the mind to dwell on questions that are unprofitable in themselves or else entirely beyond its grasp." Babbitt contended that no critical pursuit can ever be genuine if in any way it surrenders to Rousseau's counsel, "Let us begin by setting aside all the facts." The germs of Babbitt's criticism are social and moral in direct relation to his fundamental concern with the eclipse of the idea of value in modern literature—and civilization. The theory and the practice of criticism require concentration and selection, even in those same contexts that Babbitt respects in Joubert's view of religion: "Religion is neither a theology nor a theosophy; it is more than all that: a discipline, a law, a yoke, an indissoluble engagement." Far from making a "war on literature," as his detractors charged, Babbitt examined the experience of literature as ethical and moral experience. He refused to place criticism in an aesthetic or metaphysical vacuum. The critic reveals his moral sense and validates his relevance through a dedication to standards. Criticism must be a "faith free from illusion."

For his seriousness and commitment Babbitt dared the displeasure of the greater powers. His own university was neglectful in its treatment of him. In particular his feud with the "philological syndicate" was painful and damaging. His categorization of senior colleagues as "intellectual voluptuaries" who "philologize everything" and sacrifice judgment and selection to "the excess of dry analysis and fact-collecting"; his attacks on Harvard's President Charles W. Eliot for breaking down educational tradition in favor of humanitarian conceptions; his indictment of the study of literature as being "rather aimless and just a bit unmanly"; his demand that Ph.D. study, which he saw as an imitation of German scholarship, be rehabilitated so as to include a "right training in ideas"—in all these contentions Babbitt no doubt provoked the "super-professors" and gained the enmity of the academic establishment.

At a crucial point in Babbitt's life it was not quite certain that he would even be able to go on with his teaching. "I wonder how long," he writes to More in 1910, "Harvard will continue its present policy of giving me first-rate responsibility with second-rate recognition." One has a strong sense of his deepening isolation as a result of the "warfare of principles" to which he was committed. Sinclair Lewis's mocking of the "chilly enthusiasms" of the New Humanists is typical of the critical opinion which

Babbitt had to confront. Today it is not unusual for the literary politicians of revolution to single him out as a "suzerain of [an] elite-university literature department." Yet, whatever the virulence of the attacks on him or the unpopularity of the principles for which he struggled, Babbitt did not weaken: "I should prefer never to get any recognition at all than to get it by flattering the enormous humanitarian illusions of the age."

When so many other teachers and critics were, as they are still, involved in propagating the gospel of progress and reform, Babbitt strived to submit all the important issues to "a perfectly pitiless dialectic." To this dialectic he gave a stylistic form not unlike that which he praised in Hippolyte Taine, "real virility of thought and expression." The style, like the man, reflected a growth in assurance, unfailing in its commitment to principles of order, discipline, control. Characteristically, Babbitt remained adamant against appeals from some of his followers to open his "circle of ideas" so that he would attract more sympathizers. "Smartness and journalistic over-emphasis" he refused, seeing these as constituents of the leveling process that he coupled with surrender to a "cheap contemporaneousness."

One cannot appraise Babbitt's writings in chronological order. His books have a concentric design. They form an unbroken circle; and they become, intellectually, morally, and emotionally, a configuration, returning always to his central idea of life. One could as easily begin with *On Being Creative* (1932) as with *Literature and the American College* (1908). There is no pattern of development and inner changes in Babbitt's criticism; in this connection, More remarks: "He seems to have sprung up, like Minerva, fully grown and fully armed. No doubt he made vast additions to his knowledge and acquired by practice a deadly dexterity in wielding it, but there is something almost inhuman in the immobility of his central ideas."[12] Babbitt's criticism as a whole announces, repeats, and returns to fundamental tenets. There is not really a clear line of demarcation between his essays and books—between his fugitive pieces (articles, reviews, review-essays) and his collections of essays. Throughout there is a concentrated and a recurrent insistence on, rather than an expanding movement of, criticism as "a discipline of ideas." Analytical argument forms the substance of and gives momentum to his criticism, delighting in repartee and written in a masculine, sometimes racy and aphoristic style. Protest and warning inform the intensity of his critical judgments and contemplations.

Babbitt was inescapably aware of evil and the antithetic vices. And though he is a critic and not a prophet, it is equally true that his criticism, as an exercise of judgment and a judgment of value, is prophetic in its insistent tone and its repetitive accent. His response to Rousseau and romanticism, not unlike Edmund Burke's response to Rousseau and the Jacobins, was in the nature of prophecy: the response of a critic's whole being, rational and emotional, but never abstract or scientific. Babbitt combines the critic's clarity of aim with the prophet's spiritual insight.

The act of valuation, when dictated by prudence, courage, and honor, was for him an act that stamped not only the character of an individual but also that of society. Much as it is, it is not enough to say that he was our last great teacher-saint. "Oh, Babbitt," a Hindu exclaimed to More, "he is a holy man, a great saint!"[13] That Babbitt's achievement is of the spirit is to underline an important quality of his thought. But we must be willing to go beyond even this to discover the source of his real importance: that his criticism is an expression of the spirit, its offshoot and concomitant, all the more to be admired for loyalty to "the permanent things" in a time of distraction and dissolution. Even this late in the season and in this most unpropitious of times, we may say straight out that Babbitt stands among the masters of modern American criticism.

## CHAPTER TWO

# The Critical Mission

## I

"Fighting a whole generation is not exactly a happy task," wrote Irving Babbitt, recognizing the painful costs of his mission as a teacher and critic. These are brave words not often heard in the academy, where judgments that are at once critical and moral are neither fashionable nor expedient. If uttered, they are frequently received with haughty skepticism. The critic who makes moral judgments meets with a resistance that, in amoral or immoral critical contexts, turns into acceptance or even acclamation. But if Babbitt had been seeking academic standing, he would never have written as he did. Fortunately he had more important matters to attend to than worrying about executing a calm and prosperous passage in the academic world. Neither compromise nor timidity was a quality that Babbitt ever adopted. He had hard and threatening, as well as prophetic, truths to deliver to a world that, for him, extended far beyond that of "the hustling scholar" and his "productive scholarship." Babbitt chose to be, within the educational community, something of an outsider. In time he also came to be treated as an outlaw by those academics who watch over their special provinces. The values implicit in Babbitt's teachings and writings were increasingly incompatible with those of his contemporaries. He equated their values with "the democratic absurdity" and other forms of a failure of authority—and of nerve.

Babbitt was a brave man whose example must remind us that nothing else is worth having. Perhaps one of the most extraordinary characteristics of his thought is that he was a man without doubts. Some teachers confess, reproachfully, to themselves, or perhaps to their students or to their colleagues, doubts concerning their work, or the worth of their work, or the influence of their work. Some critics, and even some great authors, come to see their writings as just so many words to be forgotten or to be preserved only for the specialists or, as Babbitt called them, "the throng of scholiasts and commentators whom Voltaire saw pressing about the outer gates of the Temple of Taste." Such confessions may come out of humility, or exhaustion, or disappointment, or uncertainty. But whatever their source, they stem from self-doubt. Feelings of meaninglessness often preclude gestures of renunciation—both for the teacher who would be a savior and for the writer who would be an evangel. For Babbitt such confessions would have constituted routes of escape and self-indulgent solace unworthy of and unwelcome to one who steadfastly taught the Socratic, the humanistic, doctrine—"the discipline of a central standard"—and who affirmed Goethe's admonition that "anything that emancipates the spirit without a corresponding growth in self-mastery, is pernicious." It could be said that Babbitt never lost his vision of the One, in the absence of which there is inevitably, as he declared, "a disquieting vagueness and lack of grip in dealing with particulars."

A man of firm confidence, he never lost his own "grip in dealing with particulars." While so many teachers, critics, and thinkers were busily questioning, even destroying, the traditional values, and at the same time creating new abstractions or avoiding valuations, Babbitt admonished that it was urgent to create "an aristocracy of character and intelligence." The act of valuation, as a courage of judgment, was for him not only a serious but also a moral matter that qualitatively affected not only the individual but also the whole of society, of civilization. In place of a policy of expansionism, he counseled one of retrenchment, hardly a popular program to recommend to a nation boastful of its optimism. He realized fully the difficulty of advocating the aristocratic principle at a time when "all the ideas which I know to be most vital for many have more and more declined." Nor did his stress on the disciplinary and selective "truths of the inner life" find favor in a secular age glorifying the gospel of progress and bigness and promising to open "the gates of Eden," as daring a promise as any that, Babbitt would go on to say, pushes pluralism to excess and assaults the supreme law of life—the law of measure. Babbitt chose to fulfill the function of the critic, which Matthew Arnold had formulated: "...whoever sets himself to see things as they are will find himself one of a very small circle; but it is only by this small circle resolutely doing its own work that adequate ideas will ever get current at all." That he would not substitute miscellaneous sympathies for firm principles of judgment; or cower before the imperial power of what he labeled "a cheap contemporaneousness"; or view the human problem as merely a socioeconomic one—these were brave refusals that distinguished Babbitt from his contemporaries.

The thrust of his judgments, enhanced by his penchant for polemics and ripostes, alienated many of his contemporaries and continues to alienate those who now sneer at him for his "one-sided erudition of doctrinaire propaganda." The animus against him, always lingering (and even at times unscrupulous), and in itself a symptomatic phenomenon, springs to attack at the mere mention of his name. Daring to speak favorably of him, especially among teachers and scholars, has a curious way of eliciting, in

print or *viva voce,* a double damnation: both of the embat-
tled defendant and of his wary defender. Babbitt's ideas
touch sensitive nerve centers. His whole critical approach,
etched as it is by strenuous self-assurance, has about it a
kind of direct and unguarded fearsomeness, pushing aside
cozy collegial loyalties engendered by the "associational
process," as Henry James once described it. Babbitt's final
goal, he wrote, was "to define types and tendencies, and
not to satirize or even label individuals." What he wanted
to show was "not that our contemporary scholars are lacking in humanistic traits, but that the scholars in whom
these traits predominate are few...." Babbitt had a way of
expressing things, of hitting the mark, with a sparseness, a
cutting simplicity, an honest severity, and a robust, even
pungent, authoritativeness. The aphoristic quality of his
writing has, unfortunately, been largely ignored. His writing was cast very much in the mold of a New England
mind preaching the New England virtues of conviction,
self-control, and good character. A sturdy, if inelegant, ser-
monic note pervades Babbitt's writing, reinforced at every
step by his desire to persuade men's intellects and to
awaken their hearts. His "sermon" possesses the plain style
of the Puritans.

Babbitt's greatest achievement, Walter Jackson Bate has
stated, was "to recall an entire academic and critical generation to consider primary questions."[1] Since 1952, when
this statement was made with rare and grateful fairness,
much has occurred in American intellectual and cultural
life to substantiate Babbitt's persistent warning that modern man is "treading very near the edge of sudden disaster."
Insofar as we are still witnessing both its concomitants and
its consequences, we find it difficult to estimate the ramifications of this disaster. Our difficulty is exacerbated by
the fact that, for many, the disaster has never happened;
possibly it only has happened for the priests and the
prophets and the moralists for whom disaster is necessar-

ily an occupational hazard. The yearning to await the promise of a "new deal" or to relay the "good news" is, for some, an unsacrificeable illusion. Yet Babbitt saw the contemplative life and the permanent things deteriorate into what he termed "a delicious epicureanism," as the need for "a juster judgment and richer selection" became a victim of "the furious and feverish pursuit of mechanical efficiency." Essentially a "destructive critic," he opposed the cock-a-hoop tendencies of modern man and called them errors. This was hardly a popular role. It never is for the critic who attempts to act as the conscience of the race. To academics Babbitt became an embarrassment, for he charged them with betraying their moral function. To critics he was an oddity, for he demanded criticism with a centrality and a direction. To the intelligentsia at large he was essentially a persona non grata, for he demanded a discipline that they could not meet.

No reader of Babbitt can come away without having gained an awareness of the qualities that shaped his mind and character. A sense of contact with a major force, a major critic, is inescapable. Even when one resists or disagrees with his ideas, one cannot dispense with them without assessing them. Babbitt has a power of forcing reaction, of requiring some kind of analytical exertion. It is not merely that he forces one to deal with overwhelming issues, but that his criticism becomes a source of reflection, as well as, in the end, a path of meditation. Babbitt's criticism is concerned with something more than the so-called business of criticism, since for him the critical pursuit transposes into the pursuit of criteria of wisdom. To read Babbitt and to discover the value of his critical mission is to be reminded of ultimate human questions—and answers. He is a severe critic whose driving force of thought and whose moral purposes are never confused about their target, possessing as they do a defiant confidence and a cosmopolitan rightness, as intimidating as they are earnest. Babbitt invariably addresses himself to the catechumen. He neither makes empty promises nor incites tempting illusions. In an age when creator and critic have been subjected both to an overriding skepticism and to a general softness of standards, Babbitt taught a doctrine of human centrality, of sentience and responsibility. What some take to be the singlemindedness, or even the narrowness, of his critical views is in reality a persevering toughness.

Babbitt was a great man in the Emersonian sense that "great men exist that there may be greater men." He was to attain and to personify the kind of disciplined transcendence that enabled him to inhabit a higher sphere of thought, a sphere to which, to quote Emerson again, "other men rise with labor and difficulty." In Babbitt one finds no tormenting paradoxes, complexities, anomalies, conundrums, or enigmas; he admits to no baffling deflections in his critical ideas. Indeed, he reveals in many and astonishing ways a mastery—a command—of analytical thought that underscores attained resolutions. Order and control, two of his principles, impel and inform his ideas. Constancy and consistency register the moral rhythm of his thought. The life and health of the mind remain his absorbing purpose. He does not explore new pathways. He is no critical adventurer. Adventure in itself he finds suspect: a Dionysian quest that too easily becomes uncertainty and dissolution. His work is not addressed to those who want a journey of discovery. One of his goals is to discourage man from distorting himself in the pursuit of the unknown—for Babbitt the epitome of fantasms, lost bearings, and "great confusion." He affirms man's need to husband his resources, to plot his way, to affirm character rather than temperament, adhering to both restraint and constraint. Babbitt's emphasis on limits is never without a recognition of the need for humility. It is the austere voice of the schoolmaster that speaks in Babbitt—a New

England schoolmaster of a nation during extreme times.

Particularly within the progressivist ethos, that which inspires the modern gospel of humanitarianism dependent on technology and pluralism on the one hand and allied to compassion and social hope on the other, finds staunch opposition in Babbitt. The continuing refusal to recognize Babbitt's significance stems in large part from a commonly held view of him as a hard, elitist-oriented "antimajoritarian." Insofar as from the turn of the century he condemned the growing obsession with socioeconomic capabilities and arrangements, he chose to reject a way of life that, especially in more recent history, is increasingly controlled—programmed, in today's parlance—by precisely the social scientists whom Babbitt early recognized as sabotaging the values of humanistic culture. In countering this movement Babbitt was challenging powerful forces ("the wave of the future"). Against them he posited what he believed to be saving principles of order, insisting that unless a sound and qualitative dialectic is able to come to the rescue, all the terms expressive of the higher values of human nature are in danger. As a teacher and critic, then, he chose to devote himself to the greater moral issues rather than to the sophomoric intellectual discourses that other academics are usually content with pursuing. It would be fair to say that Babbitt was to be another (and by no means the last) victim of the by now all too familiar alliance between academics in the liberal arts, who distrust a moral critic's diagnostic insistences, and social scientists, who detest his cultural convictions and his stress on the need for standards.

To include Babbitt's writings, so long neglected, among the major texts of American criticism, and to place Babbitt, so long relegated to an orphan status, among the major critics—among, that is, the "keen-sighted few" (to use his own term)—form a dual necessity that has been ignored. The failure to recognize Babbitt's critical contribution instances a shameful episode in the history of

American intellectual life. At a time when lesser critics amass reputations and influences in excess of their achievement or their intelligibility, it is imperative to salute Babbitt's contribution and to demand that it be given its due. Babbitt died nearly sixty-five years ago, but his critical thought is very much for our time. Yet it is not easy to rescue him from the fate assigned to him by no less than Edmund Wilson, who stated, in a letter to Burton Rascoe of April 8, 1930, "that Humanism is now a flattened corpse over which the whole army of American intelligence has passed, and that it might as well be left for dead."[2] The prejudices and fallacies inherent in Wilson's denigration are repeated just as fiercely by today's hardened literary politicians of revolution, who oppose what they see as the Arnoldian "administration" of literature and who yearn desperately for the final and irrevocable "demystification of authority." Against this prevailing climate of a new absolutism, the task of winning recognition for Babbitt's critical relevance is formidable.

But such a task is essential. Babbitt's steadfastness, in the face of an orthodoxy of messianic pragmatism, should serve as an example to those who would dare to believe that the teacher's and the critic's main goal is the achievement of a wisdom that points to positive insight, to self-mastery rather than to solipsistic self-assertion and self-liberation. For Babbitt, what is important about one, and what identifies one in the contexts of a controlling purpose and value, is whether one's point of view is Socratic or sophistic. It was this that impelled, stamped, and interrelated Babbitt's standards of judgment in his outlook and overview, in his valuation of the life of literature, and in his perception of ideas and the world. Babbitt harbored no delusion about the possibility of training the ideal critic in the modern world or of attaining standards of order that resist what he termed "the disillusion of decadence." He saw his mission as one defining and conveying corrective judicial measures. To this end he worked in the hope that "some progress might at least be made towards tempering with judgment the all-pervading impressionism of contemporary literature and life." What most characterizes Babbitt as a teacher and critic is that he spoke out. In an age that has seen the abridgement of the heroic spirit, Babbitt's willingness to face hard problems and to make discriminations provides a much needed lesson in critical conviction and courage.

## II

An unceasing vigilance characterized Irving Babbitt's mission as a teacher and critic. Whatever he observed or looked at in the human world—particularly in literature, politics, education, philosophy, and religion—he saw with a rigorous and vigorous exactness, at once perusing, inspecting, and appraising an issue in a constant critical process. In both his outlook and his overview he was painstakingly discriminating. He was not afraid to define and to pronounce his value judgments on matters that he believed profoundly affected the human fate. The need to look not only at things but also beyond them constituted for Babbitt an urgent critical responsibility. Enthusiasms and impressions of the hour, or of the season, or of the age, he dismissed as the consequences of "free temperamental overflow." At the vortex of this overflow, impelling and molding it, and as the cause of what might be termed the crisis of modern civilization, he placed Jean Jacques Rousseau. Babbitt characterized Rousseau's achievement, in its continuing influence on modern life, as immense and far-reaching. In Rousseau's contention that "man is naturally good and it is by our institutions alone that men become wicked," Babbitt pinpointed what he believed to be the "new dualism," replacing the "older dualism" and thus transferring the struggle between good and evil from the heart of man to society. In this transference Babbitt saw a portentous and epochal yielding to the sociological view of life. It was to signify a consequential shifting of standards and traditions favoring the humanitarian over the humanistic and the immediate over the transcendent. It marked the ascendancy, if not the triumph, of the vital impulse. And for Babbitt it was to mark the elimination of the principle of control, without which spiritual anarchy prevails.

Throughout his life Babbitt devoted all his energy to stressing the need for recovering spiritual discipline. He stressed that, to attain this ultimately unifying discipline, the development of a humanistic attitude was necessary. In relying on social dualism, the naturalist, he believed, was evasive and superficial in his treatment of evil; the supernaturalist, on the other hand, ultimately sought total renunciation, containing an ascetical quality that Babbitt found excessively mystical and even morbid, as well as remote from "the actual data of experience." "The right use of grace and similar doctrines," he says, "is to make us humble and not to make us morbid or discouraged."

The humanistic virtues that Babbitt proffered had as their chief aim "not the renunciation of the expansive desires but the subduing of them to the law of measure." In short, he sought to teach a humanism that he considered to be both positive and critical. Failure to recover the true dualism or its equivalent, "a reaffirmation of the truths of the inner life in some form—traditional or critical, religious or humanistic," he asserted, would have tragic consequences for civilization. In dealing with the problems of the intellect and the will, he counted as crucial the need for the definition and application of standards. The neglect and discrediting of "the analytical intellect" were disturbing developments that Babbitt located within the modern movement from Rousseau to Henri Bergson. (He was severely critical of Bergson, in whom he saw a representative of the modern thinker, "a new Protagoras," who rejoiced in novelty for its own sake, wanted nothing better than "to whirl forever on the wheel of change," and constructed a metaphysics of "intoxication with the future.")

Tied to and symptomatic of the discrediting of the analytical intellect, Babbitt further believed, was an irresponsible use of general terms. Two such terms, to which he returned repeatedly, were "classicism" and "romanticism." Babbitt's entire thought revolved around not only the use but also the informing ethos of these words, insofar as each makes concrete a "life-attitude," or an idea of value. Without an understanding of these two key words there can be no understanding of Babbitt's teaching and criticism. He believed that one's own definition and applied understanding of these words epitomize one's perception and concept of life. The nature of one's understanding, in fact, helps to identify the measure of one's own quest for meaning and value.

To Babbitt the capacity to identify the discrete qualities that characterize classicism and romanticism denoted a qualitative, critical act of responsible self-recognition, if not of self-perpetuation, and beyond that, an awareness of the very quality of civilization itself. That is to say, what one says about, the response he makes to, the weight and significance that he attaches to these words, the defining essences, requirements, possibilities, and functions that he located in each, help to determine the difference between discrimination and indiscrimination, between triumph and failure, order and chaos, civilization and barbarism. The need to distinguish between classicism and romanticism constituted, for Babbitt, a judgmental process that centers, and insists, on fundamentals: on fundamentals that must posit critical standards and discipline in an age that has witnessed the weakening of traditional beliefs. In emphasizing the need for clear-cut definitions, for precise critical analysis and "hard consecutive thinking," Babbitt hoped to bring attention to the allied need for affirming an enduring scale of values, in the permanent framework of which the job of definition and analysis must be done. "Unless a sound dialectic comes to the rescue," he warned, "all the terms expressive of the higher values of human nature are in danger of being discredited."

Romanticism the term—no less than its great evangelist, Rousseau—finds in Babbitt a formidable antagonist. Neither the definition nor the comprehension of this word can be complete without some reference to Babbitt's thoughts on the subject. His consideration of romanticism, whether as an idea or as an intellectual movement, is incessant and categorical. Babbitt was never one for shirking the burden, or the courage, of his judgment. ("All children, nearly all women and the vast majority of men always have been, are and probably always will be romantic," he wrote in words that capture that polemical and uncompromising tone, as well as that tough honesty, that permeates Babbitt's critical opinions.) In romanticism and in the romantic, Babbitt found something that is wonderful rather than probable; something that "violates the normal sequence of cause and effect in favor of adventure." In particular he detected the romantic attitude in writing, and in what he called "imaginative unrestraint," that he found synonymous with the thrilling, the marvelous, the melodramatic, and with that which leads to imagination superseding judgment and reason, in short, to "the despotism of mood."

"Romantic impressionism" is another term that Babbitt often used to pinpoint what he believed to be excesses of the imagination. "Writing that is romantic," he asserted, "writing in which the imagination is not disciplined to a true centre is best enjoyed while we are young. The person who is as much taken by Shelley at forty as he was at twenty has, one may surmise, failed to grow up." We hear in these words the voice, disciplined and disciplining, of the didactician; the fact remains that Babbitt never separated his vocation as a teacher from his mission as a critic. Closely scrutinizing the consequences of the romantic attitude, in literature as in society, he was unrelenting in his view of it as lacking sufficient qualitative discrimination and as erring inevitably on the side of emotion, and worse, of anarchy: "The romanticist...revels in the mere picturesqueness of the facts or else takes refuge in the past from the present, uses it...to create for himself an alibi. But the past should be regarded primarily neither as a laboratory for research nor as a bower of dreams, but as a school of experience."

Babbitt was fully aware that classicism can degenerate into the pseudoclassicism of the eighteenth century (when form, for instance, became formalism) and, in turn, into an artistic Pharisaism: "the romantic view...is too much the neo-classical view turned upside down," he asserted. The classicism he championed had to be a classicism of standards, in essence not local or national or relative, but universal and human. Such a classicism affirms "a general nature, a core of normal experience" and possesses an abiding element, an intrinsic, unifying principle, in the midst of the flux of circumstance. Its sources and its paradigms are in Hellenism, where, in theory and in practice, it attained its apogee. It is best revealed in and exemplified by Aristotle. Aristotle and classicism contain Babbitt's answer to Rousseau and romanticism. The Hellenic, the classical, spirit underlines the doctrine of measure, a law to which all of man's religious, ethical, and aesthetic values must finally be referred. Classicism supplies models for imitation. Ignoring or rejecting them leads to "the progressive decline of standards."

For Babbitt, then, the classical spirit emphasized the recognition of limit, whereas the romantic spirit was a yearning for the infinite. The decline of the classical spirit in the modern world, as he was to show, was not restricted merely to the decline of the moral imagination. Inevitably it instanced a much wider and more serious decline that spilled over into ethical action, into the sociopolitical realm. The end that Babbitt sought, despite the severely magisterial tone of his pronouncements (if not his fiats), was one of reconciliation appropriate to the modern age: reconciliation of the creative enthusiasm of romanticism with the disciplined strength of classicism—that achieved great middle ground where "man may combine an exquisite measure with a perfect spontaneity, that he may be at once thoroughly disciplined and thoroughly inspired."

The critic's battle against romanticism can no more cease than can the priest's battle against sin. In waging this war against inveterate and unforgiving enemies, who from the beginning attacked his work as an example of "the neo-pseudo-bluestocking variety"—"the more earnest the moralist, the more justly suspect the historian," Arthur O. Lovejoy, philosopher and critical realist, said derisively of Babbitt's interpretations—he persisted in his contention that moral contexts and moral effects are inseparable. In this respect he insisted on the operative value, the "imitation," of a standard—a standard of discrimination as well as a standard of conduct: What one says about literature and how one judges its significance and value should also tell us much about what one thinks of life. It is this moral correlation between literature and life that Babbitt posited and that challenged and unsettled those who refused to see the correlation or, if they did see it, chose to see it as a curious form of "the smuggest puritanism." In his outlook, as in his overview, Babbitt was immovably ethical. "When first principles are involved," he said, "the law of measure is no longer applicable. One should not be moderate in dealing with error." His criteria were not metaphysical dreams. In his introduction to *Rousseau and Romanticism*, considered by some critics his *chef d'oeuvre*, he wrote: "But, though strictly considered, life is but a web of illusion and a dream within a dream, it is a dream that needs to be managed with the utmost discretion, if it is not to turn into a nightmare. In other words, however much life may mock the metaphysician, the problem of conduct remains."

Analytical reason, which Babbitt viewed as belonging centrally to the humanistic level of experience (as opposed to the materialistic and the religious levels), when appealed to, distinguishes between "the law for thing" and "the law for man." In his writings, therefore, Babbitt sought "to trace main currents as a part of my search for a set of principles to oppose to naturalism." "A student of main tendencies," he planted himself, sturdily, on the humanistic plane, seeking, at the same time, "a truly ecumenical wisdom" and being, at all times, a good humanist and ethical positivist, "moderate and sensible and decent." "It is much easier for a man," he reflected, "to deceive himself and others regarding his supernatural lights than it is regarding the degree to which he is moderate and sensible and decent."

Babbitt believed that the modern mind tends to reject everything that has the appearance of being nonessential. His first published essay, "The Rational Study of the Classics," appearing in the March 1897 issue of *The Atlantic Monthly*, decried some of the trends he detected in higher education, especially the movement away from the classics in particular and away from the Hellenic spirit in general, and the emphasis on specialization. The latter, he claimed, was a crude American imitation of the German scientific spirit. And for the rest of his life he kept on hammering at the trends that lead to a loss of intellectual symmetry and a sense of proportion. "Men have recently shown their fitness for teaching the humanities by writing theses on the ancient horse-bridle and the Roman doorknob," he scornfully and prophetically declared. Focusing on the study of philology, which he saw as diminishing the critical role of the study of classical literature, he warned of the damaging effects of "an epidemic of pedantry": "In the classics more than in other subjects, the fact should never be forgotten that the aim proposed is the assimilation, and not the accumulation, of knowledge." Echoing Emerson, Babbitt maintained that the goal of the true scholar, and of the whole educational task, is to combine analysis and synthesis. If the European man, he noted, is sometimes excessively tied to the past, the American is unduly absorbed in the present.

Addressing himself to the progressivist and pragmatist, Babbitt sought to show that "movement is not necessarily progress, and that the advance in civilization cannot be measured by the increase in the number of eighteen-story buildings." He believed that the study of classical literature (in its historical and comparative contexts) should alert us to causes leading to the greatness or the decline of an ancient society. In the end it should help us to grasp the essences of a moral discipline, those ordering and civilizing virtues of restraint and proportion without which one's mind and character cannot be effectively formed.

"The Rational Study of the Classics" was later to be included as a chapter in Babbitt's first book, *Literature and the American College: Essays in Defense of the Humanities.* Charles Eliot Norton, American scholar and man of letters, praised this book in these words: "It is a great misfortune for us nationally that the tradition of culture is so weak and so limited. In this respect the advantage of England is great. But I hail such a book as Mr. Babbitt's as an indication of a possible turn in the tide...." For some readers, especially humanist educators, this book has always been Babbitt's most tempered, his "best and most finished piece of writing," according to Paul Elmer More. That it should inspire admiration is not difficult to understand. Containing the seeds of Babbitt's whole critical thought, it argues in favor of literary, as opposed to scientific and utilitarian, studies. But literary study, Babbitt also stipulated, must be conducted selectively and discriminatingly—always one of his central tenets; ultimately, too, it must have a formulating reference to absolute standards of literary values. His ideal of the educated man, of the *honnête homme*, was humanistic: a man morally responsible and intellectually responsive; exclusive and select in his sympathy and tastes; keenly aware of a scale of values. Education, Babbitt declared, must revolve around an integrating principle of concentration and selection, as well as of assimilation and reflection, if it is not to capitulate to the evils of specialism or to the centrifugal tendencies in human nature. Education and *humanitas* were, for Babbitt, consubstantial.

It was as a diagnostician of cultural decay that Babbitt fulfilled his roles as teacher and critic. Diagnosis, however, was not his sole or combative humanism, even as his books have been described as "so many combats all full of honorable contention." Though essentially he aimed his attention at the American scene, he was not a provincial critic in the least, but a generalist whose achievement takes on universal qualities of wisdom, as well as of vision—vision of order. He formed his diagnoses and waged his battles on the basis of his reading of and reflection on ancient, medieval, and modern literatures. A favorite phrase of his (from Matthew Arnold), "the imperious, lonely thinking power," best expresses the depth and intensity of Babbitt's examinations of the human situation. That his "system" is stringent, that he perhaps lacked appreciation of the gentler virtues, that love was not a word he used fondly or delicately are aspects of his thought that cannot be ignored. He made no pretense of denying either the stringency or the toughness of his position. "I should define myself as a realist according to the human law," he averred. His final stress was on the discipline of the mind and of the will, "the type of will that can alone raise one above the naturalistic level." He was not an idealist in the Wilsonian sense or even in the Platonic sense, as he freely admitted; he never failed to point out how "we are altruistic in our feelings about ourselves and imperialistic in our practice." To get rid of the selective and aristocratic principle, as the equalitarian democrat wanted, he warned, would create the cult of commonness. One must distinguish, Babbitt insisted, between the *hombre medio* and the *honnête homme*—between the man who makes for a chaos of values and the man who seeks a discipline of standards.

## III

Literature and life, Babbitt insisted, are indivisible: literary studies need to be justified on cultural and disciplinary grounds. The study of literature must, in effect, become a discipline of ideas: a discipline that must distinguish between significant and insignificant literature, between literature that has an ethical or moral center and literature that is subservient to the flux of relativism. Babbitt saw literary studies as an integral part of the larger educational process, specifically of the "old education" aiming for a humanistic training for wisdom and not for a humanitarian training for service and power. In this respect his critical aims can best be termed sapiential rather than sociological. He sought quality and standards and not quantity and ideals. Insofar as he regarded the modern age as revolutionary and expansionist, with the traditional supports disappearing in society, he believed that the qualitative and selective idea in cultural life must be sustained. In the study of literature, as in the whole of education, he saw a common problem that relates to the even greater crisis of modern civilization. "What seems to me to be driving our whole civilization toward the abyss at present is a one-sided conception of liberty, a conception that is purely centrifugal, that would get rid of all outer control and then evade or deny openly the need of achieving inner control." Without a sufficiently stringent discipline of ideas, Babbitt believed, the temper of the sham "liberals" would triumph, spurning the past and barely tolerating the present—"the true home of their spirit is that vast, windy abode, the future." The main task of education, and of the teacher of literature, as he envisioned it, was that of defining general terms; the ideas for which the terms stand should be studied positively, critically, and concretely, especially as reflected in major literary currents and works.

For Babbitt the critic's central task, no less than the teacher's, was one of selection and judgment, and only secondarily one of comprehension and sympathy. That the final test of art is not its originality but its truth to the universal constituted for Babbitt a transcendent standard of criticism. Particularly in nineteenth-century art and literature did he detect eccentric and centrifugal, even pathological, tendencies. He felt that these tendencies, continuing into the twentieth century, signaled a rejection of those representative qualities of vision (and of permanence) that he found in ancient Greece: "The original man for the Greek was one who could create in the very act of imitating the past. Greek literature at its best is to a remarkable degree a creative imitation of Homer." Above all he thought that original genius must not allow the synthesizing process of humility and decorum to be outstripped by temperamental excesses of self-expression and restless self-concern. Babbitt thought it important that a work be assessed not in terms of the fulfillment of a particular aesthetic aim but in terms of whether its aim is intrinsically valuable in relation to achievement and intelligibility. The main business of the critic must be one of rating "creation with reference to some standard set above his own temperament and that of the creator." Original genius must rise to ethical standards and be disciplined to reality: "Once eliminate the high impersonal standard, the ethical norm that sets bounds to the eagerness of the creator to express himself, and the eagerness of the creator to thrill to this expression, and it is hard to see what measure of a man's merit is left save his intoxication with himself, and this measure would scarcely seem to be trustworthy."

The role of the "ethical imagination," insofar as it possesses a literary conscience, or high seriousness in the Aristotelian sense, was for Babbitt a defense against the lures of "decadent aestheticism." Relentless in his censure of "romantic eleutheromaniacs," "the corrupters of the conscience in general," he held that "we must begin by creating standards." A reverence for boundaries and limits was, for Babbitt, essential; he endorsed fully Goethe's words that in limitations one first shows himself the master. But in much of modern art and literature, he argued, expression triumphs over form, a process that he associated with the Rousseauistic view of art. Such a view he saw as leading to a breakdown of standards: "There is no place in the process for the sharply drawn line of demarcation, for the firm and fast distinction. Definite standards are swallowed up in a universal relativity." The creator's need to mediate between "the outward push of expression" and "the circumscribing law" remained for Babbitt (and for "those who have thought correctly about art") a crucial one, particularly if beauty is to be acquired that is pertinent to a man. The need for mediation, in its achievement and in its truth, underlined Babbitt's view of extremes that are barbarous. Form and symmetry, then, he cited as properties essential to beauty. The epithet "beautiful," he emphasized, must not be applied indiscriminately. A sky-scraper, he noted, is hardly beautiful: "Now sky-scrapers may be picturesque, or vital, or what you will, though they are usually not much more than a mixture of megalomania and commercialism."

If Babbitt was concerned with first principles, he was also concerned with final directions. That is, he was fearful of the dehumanization of life and literature in the absence of absolute principles. In Oscar Wilde and Paul Verlaine, for example, he saw the Rousseauistic side of romanticism: "The latest romanticists have discredited themselves, which is not perhaps a serious matter; but they have also thrown a certain discredit on art and literature, and this is far more serious." For Babbitt there was no special mystery or paradox regarding the genres and the boundaries of art: "...a clear-cut type of person, a person who does not live in either an emotional or intellectual muddle, will normally prefer a clear-cut type of art or literature."

And always, too, it was the ancient Greeks to whom Babbitt referred for our emulation: to their redeeming way of mediating between the One and the Many; to their intrinsic forms of "vital unity, vital measure, vital purpose"; to their high standards of art, which at its best is a triumph of restraint. The law of measure, as taught by Aristotle, should be, first and always, the impelling principle of life and literature. In life it helps us to distinguish the congruity between appearance and reality; in literature it acts as a defense against the excesses of the romantic imagination, and particularly of the romantic religion of love: "There is in fact no object in the romantic universe—only subject. This subjective love amounts in practice to a use of the imagination to enhance emotional intoxication, or if one prefers, to the pursuit of illusion for its own sake." All this leads, Babbitt felt, to the confusion of ethical values, found, for example, in William Hazlitt, who "converts criticism itself into an art of impassioned recollection," with "its cult of Arcadian illusion and the wistful backward glance to the vanished paradise of childhood and youth when illusion was most spontaneous."

In the literature of the modern world, as in life, Babbitt perceived the consequences of a human situation when "things are in the saddle and ride mankind." For the individual and for society the consequences epitomize anarchy. The critic, and especially the moral critic, Babbitt believed, is in a position to resist and to diminish tendencies and habits of mind. Precise analysis, clear definitions of general terms, firm application of fixed principles and standards, keen awareness of the value of traditional beliefs: these are some of the qualities that a critic must bring to bear in pursuit of his task. Matthew Arnold exemplified for Babbitt precisely the pursuit of the critical function that he himself sought to fulfill in America: "Arnold always assumes a core of normal experience, a permanent self in man, and rates a writer according to the degree of his insight into this something that abides through all the flux of circumstance, or, as he himself would say, according to the depth and soundness of this writer's criticism of life." (At the same time Babbitt did not fail, as his most famous student, T.S. Eliot, did not fail, to point to Arnold's inability to rise far enough above the naturalistic level in his dealings with religion.)

Arnold had worked out a positive and critical humanism, pertinent, Babbitt averred, to the modern concepts of democracy. Thus he saw in Arnold a critic who was ahead not only of his own time but also of ours: "Not to get beyond the idea of material organization as a remedy for moral anarchy is still to linger in the zones of illusion peculiar to the nineteenth century." Arnold's belief in a high quality of leadership, in terms of secured (and secure) standards and discipline, through the interaction of education and government, is also the belief that Babbitt argues for in his *Democracy and Leadership*. The real enemy of democracy is anarchy, and the corrective of anarchy is not a material and naturalistic efficiency but a humanistic or religious discipline. To have such a discipline, Babbitt noted, there must be standards, but in order to attain standards there must be critics who are concerned with defining and applying them. To be sure, he confessed, "We have no end of clever people, but clever people without standards."

Babbitt considered Arnold's essay on Joseph Joubert "one of the best critical essays ever written in English." Babbitt was sparing in outbursts of admiration; he was not, as has been observed, "an easy prey to imaginative enchantment of any kind." His standards were usually so strict that he excluded more than he included when passing judgment and assigning value. With Arnold, he recognized in Joubert a great critic, at once simple, brave, studious, and severe; one who, as Arnold wrote in the very last sentence of his essay, "nourished on some secret tradition, or illumined, perhaps, by a divine inspiration, kept aloof from the reigning superstitions, never bowed to the gods of Canaan." Joubert, Babbitt said, possessed a true spirituality, "far removed from a man like Coleridge who retired from his actual obligations into a cloud of opium and German metaphysics." Babbitt's estimation of Joubert appears in *Masters of Modern French Criticism*, which, as Babbitt described it in his preface, is a criticism of critics.

The sieving discussion of Joubert (and of other leading French critics of the nineteenth century, *e.g.*, Chateaubriand, Sainte-Beuve, Taine, Brunetière) shows Babbitt at his best as a literary critic. His qualities of mind and of critical discrimination, of style, methodology, and scholarship, are immediately evident and provide an index to the integrity of his achievement, as well as a rebuttal of repeated charges by his detractors that he was an unsound critical thinker and a petulant writer. ("Professor Babbitt frowns a good deal and thrusts viciously," claimed one commentator.) His combination of courage of judgment and pithiness of statement radiates throughout this essay (and throughout the book itself). He never indulges in the kind of uncritical praise that, in Babbitt's own words, becomes "too full of admiration for unregulated sympathy": "Joubert tends to see only the benefits of order just as Emerson tends to see only the benefits of emancipation. In the name of what he conceives to be order, he would be too ready to deliver society over to the Jesuits and fix it in a sort of hieratic immobility." Perhaps no two consecutive sentences could better illustrate Babbitt's mastery of words or his powers of condensation and concentration. What Joubert wrote of himself can also be applied to Babbitt: "If there is a man tormented by the accursed ambition to put a whole book in a page, a whole page in a phrase, and that phrase in a word, it is I."

If Joubert leaned too much on the side of reaction in his politics and religion, he nevertheless preserved, as Babbitt emphasized, remarkable poise and balance in his literary opinions: "He did not, like so many moderns, go mad over the powers of suggestiveness." Joubert exemplified the merits that Babbitt required of a judging mind and that raise the art of criticism above impressionism and relativity. He knew how to combine sympathy with selection; how to temper expansion by concentration—"Joubert has not a trace of our modern megalomania." Babbitt called him "the critics' critic much as Spenser has been called the poets' poet" and recognized his remarkable literary perceptiveness: "Like Emerson he possessed the gift of vision, 'the eye of the spirit, the instinct of penetration, prompt discernment; in fine, natural sagacity in discovering all that is spiritual.'" Babbitt valued in Joubert the critic as sage, who joins to his sense of unity a fine perception of the local and impermanent. His overall quality as a critic is revealed by the fact that he had standards but held them fluidly. He was willing to concede much to the element of relativity without seeing literature merely as an expression of society or as the reflection of mobile conditions. Joubert perceived an "enduring something in man and aimed at it"; he focused on abiding relations. *("Il y a quelque chose d'immuable dans l'homme!")* In short, Joubert exemplified both humanistic criticism and the dignity of criticism. In his appraisal of Joubert, Babbitt offered a "collective criticism," not only a theory of criticism but also a theory of conduct, a theory of education, and a philosophy.

In art as in criticism, Babbitt contended, one must always be on guard against the impressionism that culminates in "the fatality and finality of temperament." The impressionist cancels the principle of judgment; he slides into a quagmire of illusion and relativity. To counter the existing conditions that conduce such a vulgarization of sensibility, Babbitt appealed on an international scale to "the judgment of the keen-sighted few": "What we are seeking is a critic who rests his discipline and selection upon the past without being a mere traditionalist; whose holding of tradition involves a constant process of hard and clear thinking, a constant adjustment, in other words, of the experience of the past to the changing needs of the present." He pointed to Emerson as a model of this critical spirit, as one who can help us delineate critical standards, despite the fact that Emerson also contains a baffling blend of Rousseauism ("in denying intrinsic evil in human nature") and of insight. ("The oversoul that Emerson perceives in his best moments is the true oversoul and not the undersoul that the Rousseauist sets up as a substitute.")

The "humanistic Goethe," the Goethe who renounced Rousseauistic reverie and turned from dreaming to doing, is still another model of one who can initiate us into the critical habit. In Goethe, Babbitt saw a modern who taught man the need to live and to think on the human path, one who attained and personified that existential wisdom for which Babbitt himself always sought. The problem of finding discipline and standards comprised for Babbitt the modern predicament, analogous, if one is to conceive fully its ramifying difficulties and results, to the problem that faced Socrates and the ancient Sophists: how to "recover that firm foundation for human life which a misuse of the intellectual spirit was rendering impossible."

Clearly Babbitt must be viewed as a generalist critic comparable to Carlyle, Arnold, and Emerson—inferior to them, as it is sometimes claimed, in literary quality, but superior in intellectual depth. "He is a defender of tradition, an historian of ideas and tendencies, a moralist, a popularizer of general ideas: anything and everything, in fact, except a critic or a student of criticism." So wrote a distinguished American literary critic, J.E. Springarn, in 1913, his words epitomizing the charge so often leveled at Babbitt: that he had no aesthetic theory and failed to answer the central questions: What is art? What is literature? What is criticism? Spingarn, who undoubtedly spoke for many others, objected not to Babbitt's cultural value, which he found considerable, but to his aesthetic theory, which he claimed "is vitiated by moralistic and intellectualistic errors."

Above all, Spingarn continued, Babbitt shows his "confusion of ethical bias with aesthetic thought": "He does not care what art or criticism is, but he does care that young men and women should have discipline, training, tradition, ideals." Babbitt does not see, according to Spingarn, that "disciplined art and undisciplined art are both art; or perhaps we should say that disciplined minds as well as undisciplined ones may express themselves in art." In short, what Spingarn and other opponents of Babbitt's method emphasized is that Babbitt's literary approach, in appealing to formulas, can be rejected at the same time that his ethical outlook can be praised. Babbitt was dismissed as doctrinaire, or pseudoclassic, as insensitive to the literary experience. Later another critic, perpetuating Spingarn's objections, was to write of Babbitt: "...his literary criticism was inquisitorial, shrill—criticism *manquée*—because he sacrificed aesthetic to ethical vision." Even admirers of Babbitt's critical ethos, of literary criticism that sees the continuation of literary questions into general questions, voiced the fear that a critical practitioner, by placing moral edification above appreciation of genius, might lose his detachment and become too much a servant of his mind.

"Experience...has other uses," Babbitt maintained, "than to supply furnishings for the tower of ivory; it should control the judgment and guide the will; it is in short the necessary basis of conduct." That he equated the sense of beauty with the moral sense; that his literary standards were ethical absolutes, involving a violation of immediacy; that he "fatally" separated two orders of intuitions, the sensuous or aesthetic from the spiritual or intellectual; that he placed inordinate stress on control of the artistic imagination; that he expounded his views with "a feverish quickstep that arises from almost an excess of earnestness":—these are summary charges continually brought against Babbitt. To some extent these charges are valid, but they are valid only if one decides to separate Babbitt as literary critic from Babbitt as social critic, a separation that he himself never condoned.

The fact remains that Babbitt viewed, and appraised, literary situations as cultural situations. In the process he damned much, whether in art or in criticism, in the name of standards, an act that must be taken into account in weighing the charges against him. "There are critics who have founded," he wrote, "a considerable reputation on the relationship that exists between their own mediocrity and the mediocrity of their readers." In his view of the critical function there was obviously no room for endearing diplomacy and niceties. The critical act of judgment—and a judgment is personal or it is nothing—requires a mental toughness that is both a rejection of "unprofitable subtleties," to use Bacon's term, and a refusal of elegance: "The significant struggle is between the sound and the unsound individualist." For the modern critic, Babbitt contended, the main problem was how to "escape from the quicksands of relativity to some firm ground of judgment." He had little tolerance for *dilettantes* and *jouisseurs littéraires,* leading one critic to observe, "...Babbitt never takes a holiday. There is 'work' to be done, ethical work, seven days a week."

## IV

Irving Babbitt was a man of ideas, which he held to resolutely once he had evaluated and assimilated and then converted them into principles. His younger Harvard colleague, the critic Theodore Spencer (1902-1949), always remembered Babbitt as a brave illustration of one who knew how to use ideas as principles. "His opinion was a foundation—it was as solid as a piece of granite," Spencer observed. Even in his writing the tenacity of Babbitt's ideas and opinions was one of his most identifiable, even overriding, traits. "He wrote always not for display but for conviction," Paul Elmer More has remarked. But whatever the tenacity of his ideas, Babbitt never failed to discover hidden relationships between historical or literary ideas. He looked on the exchange of ideas as essential, though at the same time he insisted on value. "There can be no assigning of values except in terms of ends," he said, "and no discovery of universal ultimate values except in terms of universal ultimate ends." Consequently he was to echo Matthew Arnold's rejection of the "over-preponderance of single elements": a rejection, that is, of the claims of a Romantic monism.

Babbitt insisted on the discipline of ideas and not on the adventure in ideas, or indeed, on the "adventure of ideas," to borrow Alfred North Whitehead's phrase. He never stopped trying to relate what he believed to be positive and critical to the modern world. What he saw all around him, and attacked, was a rampant, an "imperialistic" (to use his own word), secularism: a world, he believed, in which the central maxim of the humanists, ancient and modern, "Nothing too much," was in eclipse. "In the ancients we should look for beauties because we frequently miss these," he said. "In contemporaries we should see faults, for they are part of the very air we breathe, the *Zeitgeist,* and we are in danger of not noticing them." His teachings and writings, then, were both corrective and catechetical. How can modern man convert the idea of value into the life of value? For Babbitt, this was a paramount question that tended to be sidetracked, ignored, scorned.

To preserve the integrity of the inner life, Babbitt claimed, it is necessary to set up a world of entities, essences, or "ideas" above the flux. The idea of self-reliance is, in this regard, all-important, requiring the possession of sound standards and the freedom to act on them. To secure standards one needs intellect, that power in man that analyzes, discriminates, and traces causes and effects. To act on them one needs will. "Spiritual strenuousness" was one of Babbitt's principles of life, and it was his final answer to the utilitarian-sentimental confusion of values and also his equivalent of passion. ("Love is the fulfilment of the law and not, as the sentimentalist would have us believe, a substitute for it.") One's moral conscience, Babbitt maintained, can never be replaced by social conscience. The distinction between one's moral and social, or material, progress can hardly be overemphasized. Its presence leads to making sharp exclusions and discriminations, to principles and practices and examples that positively activate civilized life and thought and that instance and confirm what Babbitt termed the "higher will": "To give the first place to the higher will is only another way of declaring that life is an act of faith." Civilization, which depends on the forms of inner action, "is something that must be deliberately willed;

it is not something that gushes up spontaneously from the depths of the unconscious."

It is true, confessed Babbitt, that modern civilization has witnessed considerable material progress. But this form of progress does not necessarily promote moral progress; it even works against it, impoverishing the truths of the inner life in their traditional forms. As a result the idea of liberty has become confused, "to be conceived expansively, not as a process of concentration, as a submission to or adjustment to a higher will." The consequence of this confusion is, for Babbitt, catastrophic for the modern world inasmuch as there is a failure to attain adequate equivalents for the traditional controls. Standards of selection are surrendered in the name of "nature," even as the ethical will gives way to a "diffuse, unselective sympathy": "This tendency to put on sympathy a burden it cannot bear and at the same time to sacrifice a truly human hierarchy and scale of values to the principle of equality has been especially marked in the democratic movement, nowhere more so perhaps than in our American democracy."

Particularly in the American achievement of his, and our, time, Babbitt detected some alarming features. If in romanticism he saw the literary expression of naturalism, in democracy he saw its political expression, which is the subject of his *Democracy and Leadership,* a book belonging to the fields of political and social science, in many ways containing a summary of Babbitt's thought and in some ways his most important contribution. Characterized by a perfect dialectic integrity, *Democracy and Leadership* is his most hardhitting, perhaps even his most threatening book, particularly in the chapter entitled "Democracy and Standards." It is the lack of standards, Babbitt claimed, that condemns the American experience to an expansive "frontier psychology."

In no way did Babbitt shirk looking at issues foursquare; he certainly did not try to flatter his readers. It is to the mind, not to the heart, that he spoke; his polemical approach, inherently lucid and robust, never wavered, based as it was on first principles—on truths. Consider these statements: "When the element of conversion with reference to a standard is eliminated from life, what remains is the irresponsible quest of thrills." "The American reading his Sunday paper in a state of lazy collapse is perhaps the most perfect symbol of the triumph of quantity over quality that the world has yet seen. Whole forests are being ground into pulp daily to minister to our triviality." "People will not consent in the long run to look up to those who are not themselves looking up to something higher than their ordinary selves." Obviously, such statements were hardly designed to endear Babbitt to his critics. Reviewing *Democracy and Leadership* in *The New Republic,* a needling T. V. Smith (1890-1964), self-styled defender of "the liberal temper" and advocate of the principle of compromise as "the very moral genius of America," wrote: "... further notice of such a book in critical circles would need apology were it not so thoroughly representative of any number of wisdom books now issuing from the citadel that humanism has erected on the banks of our democratic stream as an asylum for retired aristocrats."

It is the business of the critic, Babbitt stated, to distinguish between things that are at the center different and to apply standards of judgment. He saw the "general will" and the "divine average" as false criteria. "The unit to which all things must finally be referred is not the State or humanity or any other abstraction, but the man of character. Compared with this ultimate reality, every other reality is only a shadow in the mist." The hope of civilization, he believed, resides in the saving remnant, which must be Socratic in its dialectic. In the end, he insisted, democracy will have to be judged by the quality of its leadership.

What Babbitt especially saw as a crucial problem facing political democracy and leadership was that of placing rights before duties: "The proper remedy for an unsound individualism is a sound individualism, an individualism that starts, not from rights, but from duties." Government, he said, is power, and whether power is ethical or unethical depends finally on the quality of will disclosed by the leaders who administer the power. "The value of political thinking is therefore in direct ratio to its adequacy in dealing with the problem of power." In *Democracy and Leadership,* then, Babbitt was not afraid to identify fundamental problems that make for uncomfortable reading: "It is growing only too evident, however, that the drift towards license is being accelerated rather than arrested by the multiplication of laws."

The problem of standards and leadership, as Babbitt was always careful to indicate, is not merely an American phenomenon; it must be placed against the larger background of "slow yielding in the whole of the Occident of traditional standards, humanistic and religious, to naturalism." In many respects *Democracy and Leadership* returned to the basic issues in *Rousseau and Romanticism.* The configurative schema is an endemic feature of Babbitt's writings; he inevitably revealed the whole of his work in each of its parts. In his evaluation of Madame de Staël, he focused on her as a representative of an age expansive in taste and tendency and neglectful of discipline. Babbitt's view of her work is particularly revealing for its discussion of nationalism as a product of romanticism. In her concept of the relation of nationalities to one another he saw reproduced on a large scale the Rousseauistic conception of the proper relation of individuals: "The first law for nationalities as for individuals is not to imitate but to be themselves."

Babbitt admitted that Madame de Staël appears as the ideal cosmopolitan who has done much to advance the comparative study of literature. Yet in her cosmopolitanism he found her most pervasive and dubious trait, her romantic enthusiasm, which led him to demur: "When individual or national differences are pushed beyond a certain point what comes into play is not sympathy but antipathy." "The modern cosmopolitan is to be blamed not for developing on a magnificent scale the virtues of expansion but for setting up these virtues as a substitute for the virtues of concentration." He agreed with Madame de Staël that it is excellent to be internationally comprehensive and sympathetic, but he also noted that, unless a new discipline intervenes to control the expansion, "cosmopolitanism may be only another name for moral disintegration." True cosmopolitanism, Babbitt declared, must be a mediation between extremes; must possess the centripetal force, "the allegiance to a common standard, that can alone prevail against the powers of individual and national self-assertion."

For Babbitt the passion for humanity that marked the dawn of the French Revolution was to culminate, nationally and internationally, in imperialism. The will to power was to prevail over the will to brotherhood. He believed that nothing was easier than to transfer the concept of free expansion from the temperament of the individual to the temperament of the nation. Humanitarian devices for lessening international friction Babbitt counted as useless, insofar as "men are not governed by cool reflection as to what pays, but by their passions and imagination." (He was fond of asserting, "the progress of modern culture is from humanity through nationality to bestiality.")

The gap between human aspiration and human achievement remained for Babbitt a permanent aspect of the condition of life that utterly belies the belief of "enlightened" philosophers that the state of nature is Arcadia. As he wrote with special reference to the Great War of 1914-1918, "An age that thought it was progressing towards Armageddon suffered, one cannot help surmising, from some fundamental confusion in its notion of progress." He saw a certain likeness, in fact, between the Great War and the Peloponnesian War, "both wars of commercial and imperialistic expansion." In the Peloponnesian War the various Greek states exhausted each other to the advantage of Macedon. "In the same way," he goes on to observe—and his observation, it seems, has now transcended to prophecy—"the countries of Western Europe may exhaust one another to the ultimate advantage of a comparatively uncivilized Power—Russia." Babbitt never weakened in his belief that "the present imperialistic drift" could be checked by a recovery of the disciplinary virtues, the virtues of concentration, and the right use of the critical spirit—and "the inspired and imaginative good sense that one actually finds in the great poets and the sages." He did not fail to point out, too, that "the opposition between imagination and common-sense is one of the most vicious assumptions of the modern movement."

The national character of a people—the directions it takes, the habits of mind it discloses, the sensibility it asserts—fascinated Babbitt, alert as he was to ethical and moral dimensions. Particularly in the Spaniards did he discover the "intense play of light and shade," "the alternations of energy and inertia,...sudden vicissitudes of greatness and decay." He found lacking, or at least uncultivated, in Spain the intermediary elements of lucidity, good sense, and critical discrimination. The absence of a temperate imagination he found especially regrettable. His early essay on the Spanish character, published in 1898, is one of Babbitt's most sensitively and warmly written, the result of his own travels.[3] (Those who charge Babbitt with being too austere as a literary stylist would do well to study this essay. The equivalent charge is also sometimes made against him personally. Wyndham Lewis, who met Babbitt at Harvard in the early 1930s, helped to correct such a charge when he wrote: "I found this highly controversial professor a very wise and gentle creature indeed: if all our kind were made at all upon his model, life would certainly be less eventful, but we should have little need for extraneous 'checks,' I think.")

In this essay Babbitt combines, with exquisite balance, his ideological concern with his impressions of and insights into the Spaniard: "...he is overflowing with national pride without being patriotic. He still has in his blood something of the wild desert instinct of the Arab, and the love of personal independence of the Goth." He goes on to observe that Spain "does not share our exuberant optimism, and has misgivings about our idea of progress" and that "she is haunted at times by the Eastern sense of the unreality of life." Babbitt was disturbed, however, by Spain's choice of a guide for entering upon the path of modern progress. He believed it dangerous that, in the main, her ideas came, because of her geographical position, from France: "In that ideal cosmopolitanism of which Goethe dreamed, each country was to broaden itself by a wise assimilation of the excellencies of other nationalities. The actual cosmopolitanism which has arisen during the present century has perhaps resulted in an interchange of vices rather than of virtues." But what remains one of the most striking features of Babbitt's essay is its prophetic note, which no student of the Spanish Civil War (1936-1939) and its aftermath can overlook: "Whatever comes to pass, we may be sure that Spain will not modify immediately the mental habits of centuries of spiritual and political absolutism. In attempting to escape from the past, she will no doubt shift from the fanatical belief in a religious creed to the fanatical belief in revolutionary formulae, and perhaps pass through all the other lamentable phases of Latin-country radicalism."

Between the humanist and the humanitarian, Babbitt emphasized, there is a clash of first principles. Between the humanist and the Christian, as well as the Buddhist, on the other hand, there always exists the possibility for cooperation. As the basis of such a cooperation he indicated their common agreement on man's continual need to exercise the power of vital control, with the failure to do so constituting a chief source of evil. Humanist mediation and religious meditation he viewed only as different stages in the same ascending "path," though he also stressed that each has its separate domain. Babbitt was the first to admit that humanism cannot replace religion, that, in fact, the latter can dispense with humanism rather than humanism with religion. But at the same time, he also noted that the man who seeks to live religiously in the secular world cannot do so without referring to humanistic wisdom and some new vision of the Absolute.

Any attempt to fix a religious label on Babbitt is bound to fail, or at least to fail to convey the full extent and the deepest facets of his humanistic faith. His concern was, first and last, with the expression of human reason and not with the revelation of the supernatural. His emphasis, insofar as it touches on the religious, is moral. The rational element, in the contexts of intellect and will, rather than the sacramental is for him of final significance. It should be remembered that Babbitt found objectionable what he called the "tremendous spiritual romanticism" of Saint Augustine and that he had a strong aversion to the concepts of the fall of man found in Pascal and in Jonathan Edwards, which he characterized as extreme "expressions of the theological terror."

It was in the religious thought of the Far East that Babbitt found an absence of that warfare between reason and faith that plagued Occidental culture: "Buddha and Confucius both managed to combine humility with self-reliance and a cultivation of the critical spirit." He applauded the two great religious teachers' affirmation of the truths of the inner life and of that permanent self that exercises control. Buddha, in particular, was free from those undesirable elements so often found in the Occident: intolerance, obscurantism, and casuistry. "The greatest of the Eastern analysts," he reminded Babbitt of Aristotle, "the master analyst of the West." (His thoughts on Buddha are found in one of his most remarkable essays, "Buddha and the Occident," written in 1927 but not published until 1936, when it was included in a volume with Babbitt's translation, from the Pāli, of *The Dhammapada*. His translation has been applauded as "an inspired re-creation, the result of a long love and deep conviction.") Only a Buddha, claimed Babbitt, can apprehend the whole, possessing as he does a "rounded vision." The Buddhistic act itself is a rigorous tracing of moral cause and effect, as well as a discriminating temper appearing in the use of general terms; "vision" is synchronous with the critical act of analysis.

Babbitt admitted that Buddha's teaching is not easy for the Westerner to grasp: "Buddha is so disconcerting to us because doctrinally he recalls the most extreme of our Occidental philosophers of the flux, and at the same time, by the type of life at which he aims, reminds us rather of the Platonist and the Christian." He described Buddha as a critical and experimental supernaturalist, that is, one who starts from "the immediate data of consciousness" rather than from certain dogmatic and metaphysical affirmations about ultimate things. In consequence, Buddhism looks up to and deals with the Law, the law of control, the special law of human nature. Babbitt was careful to point out, too, that the Buddhist, like the Christian, is an uncompromising dualist for whom the problem of evil is immense and unending. As Buddha said: "That alone I have taught, sorrow and the release from sorrow." He taught, above all, the spiritual need to attain a wholeness that is related to holiness and is the result of a concentration of will.

The unity of life that Primitive Buddhism *(Hīnayāna)*

sought for, according to Babbitt, is to be achieved by an exercise of will that checks for the expansive desires and that substitutes the more permanent for the less permanent among these desires. In Buddha's assertion of this quality of will he saw the concentrated process of religious thought that belonged not to a philosophical system in the Occidental sense but to a "path." Only those questions of human existence that make for edification were allowed by Buddha. Man, he taught, must save himself. Man, in effect, cannot rely upon divine grace, or upon rites and ceremonies, in short, upon the Church and Revelation. The Buddhist quest, Babbitt stressed, is not for mere cessation but for the eternal in the form of a present blessedness to be found within the human state, the "*Nirvāna* here and now," which is attained through the right use of meditation. Buddha stands for the idea of meditation as it is irrevocably and transcendently tied to the principle of control. The meditation of the Buddhist is also tied to the exercise of the transcendent will.

In Buddhism, Babbitt also sought to show a religious movement that was free from the romantic elements of strangeness and wonder ascribed to it by Friedrich Schlegel and from the pessimism that Schopenhauer found in it. Far from being either nihilistic or pessimistic, Babbitt maintained, Buddhism was emphatically a religious ideology of earnestness, seeking at all times to defeat the forces of evil within one's self; to quell the impulses of temperament *(pamāda)*; and to induce the active exercise of control, the greatest of the virtues *(appamāda)*. Buddha, as Babbitt pointed out with assent, summarized his doctrine in one word, "strenuousness," in which all salutary conditions have their root, or as Buddha himself said: "Strenuous among the slothful, awake among the sleepers, the wise man advances like a racer leaving behind the pack."

One must be careful, Babbitt steadfastly maintained, to distinguish religion from romanticism. In early Taoism

(550-200 B.C.) he detected, and rejected, a pantheistic unity and a naturalistic and primitivistic tendency. Confucianism, he believed, contained a humanistic antidote to a romanticizing Taoism. It is not difficult to understand the reasons for Babbitt's preference. Confucian thought recognizes an eternal moral law *(tao)* that, if obeyed, lends dignity and value to human actions. It stresses that society does not exist as such but is only an extension of the individual, the result ultimately of the extension of personal virtues. It teaches the need of attaining a keen and discriminating intellect and an intellectual honesty without which there can be no moral development: "When you know a thing, say that you know it. When you do not know a thing, say that you don't know it. This is true knowledge" *(Analects,* II, 17). It insists that knowledge requires mental training and discipline; that natural desires and instincts need to be properly ordered and coordinated; that the law of inner control is the law of laws *(li),* leading to the perfected moral life *(ren).*

Since he was not a sinologue, Babbitt had to rely on translations of Chinese religious writings, a fact that no doubt made him feel somewhat of a stranger in Confucianism. (He, of course, knew Pāli, which accounts for his more detailed emphasis on Buddhism.) But clearly Babbitt understood the transcending and timeless importance of Confucianism in its idea of humility, of "submission to the will of Heaven." In this important respect, Babbitt observed, Confucius recalls Christ: "Though his kingdom is very much of this world, he puts emphasis not merely on the law of measure, but also on the law of humility." No one, Babbitt wrote, insisted more than Confucius "on a right example and the imitation that it inspires as the necessary basis of a civilized society."

Babbitt's attempt to erect "a secular philosophy of life in our time," according to T.S. Eliot, was, no matter how admirable, symptomatic of an "individualistic misdirection of will" and "a philosophy without revelation." Eliot thus summarized a basic criticism prompted by the uneasy feeling that, from a Christian perspective, humanism is incomplete. Even Paul Elmer More, Babbitt's comrade-in-arms of long standing, as well as his closest friend, was to ask toward the end of his life: "The high value of being a man—is that *telos* attainable, is it even approachable, without religion?" "Will not the humanist, unless he adds to his creed the faith and hope of religion, find himself at the least, despite his protests, dragged back into the camp of the naturalist?"[4] Eliot and More were no doubt disquieted by Babbitt's ambivalent view of the supernatural as instanced by his disavowal of "dogmatic or revealed religion."

The questions that More raised are not easy to answer, and when answers are suggested they often reflect not so much Babbitt's own position as that of the commentator. More himself, it should be pointed out, went on to trace the relations between Platonism and Christianity: in *Christ the Word* (1927) to defend Christian assumptions, and in *The Catholic Faith* (1931) to view Christianity as the complement and climax of the Greek tradition. (It should not go unnoted here that Babbitt saw as justified "the opinion of those who look upon Protestantism in all its forms as only an incident in the rise of nationalism.") Babbitt never ventured into the mystical realm, regardless of how much he esteemed orthodox Christianity, particularly the Catholic Church. More insisted that there should be no misunderstanding with respect to Babbitt's religious position: "The dogma of Grace, the notion of help and strength poured into the soul from a superhuman source, was in itself repugnant to him, and the Church as an institution he held personally in deep distaste, however he may have seemed to make an exception of the disciplinary authority of Romanism."

More's words, if too astringent, have the value of reminding us that Babbitt was not a religionist. Religious experience is not what his ideas communicate or conduce. The "self-regarding virtues," on the other hand—moderation, common sense, common decency—as mediatory forms of ethical and moral life occupy a consistently high and revered place in Babbitt's teachings. He saw that virtue is also a matter of one's personal attitude toward the world insofar as it contains the possibility of constraint, and in practice it makes for a harmony that leads to unity. In Aristotelian fashion he recognized the Law of the Mean as the secret of virtuous discipline. Virtue requires also a humanistic and critical view of life in the framework of the modern world and in the ideational contexts not of the West alone but also of the Far East, especially India and China.

Babbitt believed that, with the decline of the age of theology, the age of sociology was in ascendancy; that, with the victories of both rationalistic and emotional ethics over the traditional dualism of the eighteenth century, modern man is in the last phase of a secular process. For Babbitt this process, in all of its ramifications and consequences, was the enemy. He identified this enemy in its Rousseauistic reinterpretation of virtue as an expansive rather than as a restrictive sentiment. The values of the inner life must inevitably retreat before the imperialistic drive of such an enemy. (He stressed again and again that what in the French Revolution had started out as a humanitarian crusade ended in Napoleon and imperialistic aggression.) "The results of the material success and spiritual failure of the modern movement are before us," Babbitt wrote. He maintained that the term "modern" should be reserved for the person who strives to be critical according to both the human and the natural law. In his own ideas and in his awareness of the world Babbitt was a thoroughgoing and complete modern who did not forsake the older view of unity in diversity. This virtue of spiritual percipience made him an American sage.

## CHAPTER THREE

# Babbitt and Religion

As a teacher and critic, Irving Babbitt has come to represent a man of character, an Anglo-Saxon moralist, a New England mind, "the last of the great American Puritans." In his person, as in his teaching, Babbitt was to communicate solidity, robustness, austerity, tenacity, integrity. Even his physical appearance identified him as quintessentially Yankee: a man above average height, powerfully built, with a radiant complexion and dark blue eyes. *"Qui est ce monsieur, si beau, si distingué? Il a l'air d'un dieu!"* someone in his Parisian audience was heard to observe.[1] His was essentially a masculine disposition. Ascetical and ethereal traits are not part of this disposition; nor was there anything valetudinarian or epicurean in what he projected. Combativeness was at the center of his character and task. He was a man of immense, tactile energy: a polemical dialectician with a probative mind and prophetic message, working from axiomatic principles to inevitable conclusions. Not the idealism of Plato, but the positivism of Aristotle is what inheres in Babbitt's thought. And what is fundamental and experiential, secular and empirical in the best sense, characterizes the articles of Babbitt's humanist creed.

This creed must be assessed in the contexts of what Babbitt calls "the immediate data of consciousness," that is, those viable and verifiable elements that are distinct and different from the metaphysical and supernatural and from what he termed "a mystical-transcendental mist." In defense of his creed he was indefatigable: "Nor shall my sword sleep in my hand" are words that Babbitt might have easily written. The ancient Greeks used the adjective *gennaios* to designate a man who is high-minded, brave, manly. This word, which describes Babbitt's mission as teacher and critic, is central to "the courage to be" and "the courage of judgment." Irving Babbitt had both.

This profile can hardly do justice to the strength of conviction and "the terrible earnestness" that Babbitt disclosed in his long ministry as a teacher and critic. Even his foes paid him respect for his effort in behalf of what they happily considered to be lost causes. "He was so powerful a teacher that the very presence of him," writes Alfred Kazin in *On Native Grounds,* "the slow stubborn consecration of his ideal, was moving. In the face of so much inertia, cynicism, and triviality in others, the total absence of anything like his force in American criticism, his moral effectiveness was profound."[2]

For the most part, Babbitt has been denied full recognition as a religious man, as a man of spiritual insight. Kazin dismisses Babbitt as "a commonplace skeptic," "a Yankee Republican and a Tory materialist," who lacked religious history and religious sensibility. And Paul Elmer More, Babbitt's coadjutor and friend, opined in his obituary essay that Babbitt's life, though obedient to "the unrelenting exactions of conscience," was not a life of steady growth in Grace. "I can remember him," More reminisces, "in the early days stopping before a church in North Avenue, and, with a gesture of bitter contempt, exclaiming: 'there is the enemy! there is the thing I hate.' "[3] This incident has long influenced a common perception of Babbitt as anti-religious. Nothing could be, or has been, more misrepresentative of Babbitt's religious importance. Austin Warren defines the special nature of his mentor's saintliness by including Babbitt among the "New England Saints"—Jonathan Edwards, Ralph Waldo Emerson, Edward Taylor, Charles Eliot Norton. "My saints are," Warren emphasizes, "none of them, canonized; but they are, whether priests, and of whatever 'communion,' men I recognize, and celebrate, as those to whom reality was the spiritual life, whose spiritual integrity was their calling and vocation."[4]

But the hagiographic titles assigned to Babbitt by his Oriental admirer and his Harvard pupil have enjoyed little approval. Babbitt has always been a victim of those who, like Kazin, see him as a fanatic reactionary and those who, like F. O. Matthiessen, see his "conception of human nature …[as] high principled, but arid and inadequate."[5] These impressions of Babbitt, like More's recollection of Babbitt gesticulating at a Cambridge church, have led to a distorted image. Perhaps his friends and his enemies wanted him to be something more than he could be. To the question, "Does not criticism consist above all in comprehending?" Babbitt was to reply, "No, but in judging." That reply takes the measure of the man. It adumbrates, with economy of emotion and expression, his severe magistrative orientation and his absolute honesty. Babbitt did not fudge; there is an astonishing transparency in his total contribution that makes it difficult to accept the charge that he was plagued by "abstract spiritual manliness." What identifies Babbitt is the absoluteness and the concreteness of his views: the commitment and the pertinacity, the belief and faith, of one who avows principles of life and order. A central quality of his achievement is the absence of corruptions, of anomalies, of fantasies, of roles, of turnings. Babbitt wears no masks. The centrality of his thought is its virtue of honesty, its integrative *gennaiotēs,* to use that informing Greek word.

"The saints come to us," Henri Daniel-Rops tells us, "as the judges of their own period and society."[6] One must read Babbitt's particular form of saintliness in the contexts of these words. Daniel-Rops also reminds us that "a saint is a scandal," that he creates " 'a troublesome commotion.' " No words better characterize both the treatment and the effects of Babbitt's endeavors. But for Babbitt not to have held any one of these saintly dimensions would have made him merely another humdrum critic.

It was as a teacher-saint that Babbitt was to conduct his dedicated ministry. His arena was his classroom; his pupils were both his catechumens and his concelebrants. No other teacher in this century has more powerfully or memorably exemplified selfless commitment to the art of teaching, to *humanitas*. His writings were the products of his teaching, that is, lectures transposed from the lectern to the printed page, there to become permanent principles of character and conscience. Babbitt was to sanctify the whole process of teaching as a moral act and to elevate it to its maximum point of meaning. "Here was a new kind of teacher: not reducible to a learned expositor, he taught with authority," Warren recalls. "If, to doctrinal 'liberals,' he was patently reactionary, he defended an academic freedom precious and perishable—the freedom to judge.... He was concerned with principles, with tracing lines of intellectual development."[7] Babbitt's pupils readily testify to the greatness of his teaching, which he summarized repeatedly with his admonition, "live at the center." Even those pupils who disagreed with him and those adherents who diverted from his ideas testify to the influence Babbitt exerted on them. To read his pupils' reminiscences and tributes is to become aware of one who is, as the Chinese are wont to say, "a teacher of men." For them his classes were an intellectual and spiritual experience and, ultimately, "spiritual exercises." Master of "self-reverence, self-knowledge, self-control," he disclosed those gifts and disciplines of the teacher-saint possessing a great soul, one whom Babbitt's own master of "unsurpassed humanism," Aristotle, speaks of as *megalopsychos*.

Few would deny Babbitt recognition as a teacher-saint. But that recognition is diminished frequently by the concomitant indictment of Babbitt's humanism as being, at the very least, religiously vacuous and of Babbitt himself as being a teacher-saint who is also a heretic standing some distance from or outside of the Church and holding a position short of a commitment to Christianity. Babbitt's brand of humanism, as Marion Montgomery has charged, is overtly Hellenic and not New Testament. That is to say, Babbitt represents a gnostic mentality whereby the Greek spirit threatens to engulf faith in speculative philosophy. "Aristotle without St. Thomas," Montgomery reminds us in the course of indicting Babbitt, "like Plato without St. Paul, is an incomplete champion against secular relativism."[8] The substance of this indictment of Babbitt is not new, but goes back to what remains a definitive statement, T. S. Eliot's *After Strange Gods: A Primer of Modern Heresy* (1934), in which Babbitt is included with D. H. Lawrence, Ezra Pound, and the early Yeats as modern heretics, that is, men who are not necessarily unbelievers, but who emphasize a doctrine too strongly and obsessively, to the point of falsehood. In two earlier essays, "The Humanism of Irving Babbitt" (1927) and "Second Thoughts about Humanism" (1928), Eliot had also delineated his critique of Babbitt's religious position, or what he calls "the weaknesses of humanism."[9]

Eliot's case against Babbitt's doctrine of humanism can be summarized as follows: Insofar as humanism refuses the orthodox religious view, it seeks to be an alternative to religion; it stresses the role of human reason, not the revelation of the supernatural. As such Babbitt's humanism is essentially a byproduct of liberal Protestant theology. In the end, Babbitt is trying to make his form of humanism work without religion, even as he himself remains detached from any fundamental religious belief. Babbitt has come to know many philosophies and religions and has assimilated them so thoroughly that he cannot commit himself to any. Eliot could not accept Babbitt's emphasis on the appliance of the "inner check" in controlling the human personality's centrifugal pull. Orthodox religion alone, he insisted, was capable of providing not only the "external restraints," but also "a single spiritual core and a dogmatic creed." ("Only Christianity helps to reconcile me to life, which is otherwise disgusting," Eliot once wrote to More.) However admirable Babbitt's concern "with the discipline and training of emotion," Eliot says, the end, the *telos,* of humanism is futile: "What is the higher will to will, if there is nothing either 'anterior, or superior' to the individual?"

The depiction of Babbitt as a heretic who somehow transfigured into a moral fascist has long been with us. It has conspired to strip him of those genuine religious qualities that pervade his humanist faith and that reveal him as a great spiritual figure. If there are seeds of heresy in Babbitt, they are neither perverse nor diabolic. His heresy can be interpreted as a necessary aspect of the life of the church, as a supplement to it in the contexts of what Edmund Burke terms "the dissidence of dissent." The church and the heretics, it has been observed, form a far more vital union than either one will admit. Above all, then, the religious significance of heresy is what needs to be grasped and understood. But before examining this significance in Babbitt, it is best to earmark the major traits of a great heretic in these words of the Swiss theologian Walter Georg Nigg: "He is the extreme antithesis of the indifferentist.... He courageously accepts the consequences of his actions. His fervor can teach us the meaning of loyalty to truth. We may even say that the heretic embodies the religious spirit in concentrated form."[10]

Nigg goes on to say that the heretic typifies a repressed interpretation of religion; that unresolved problems come to life in a heretic; that a heretic seeks to advance an overlooked or misunderstood religious concept, so that religious values previously unknown are discovered. "Only great men have brought forth heresies," Saint Augustine tells us. The heretic often resembles the saint; the piety of the latter contrasts with the rebellion of the former to underscore a mission on the part of one who is simultaneously a witness, an outlaw, and even a martyr. It should be remembered that the term heresy is a transliteration of the Greek *hairesis,* meaning an act of choosing, a course of action or thought, and finally the philosophical principles of one who professes them. At its most destructive stage, heresy destroys unity and induces spiritual alienation; at its most constructive, in the words of Leopold Ziegler, heresy is "necessary for the tradition, so that it will remain in flux and not congeal into rigidity."

No less than the Blaise Pascal of the *Lettres Provinciales,* whom Unamuno termed "an orthodox heretic," Babbitt could also say, "I stand alone," as he sought to uphold the sovereignty of conscience to the point of heresy. Pascal, a religious visionary who both attracted and repelled Babbitt, was long the subject of one of his Harvard courses and much discussed in his writings. The spiritual core of Pascal's personality appealed to Babbitt, whose own religio-humanistic position is epitomized in Fragment 378 of the *Pensées*: "To leave the mean is to abandon humanity. The greatness of the human soul consists in knowing how to preserve the mean. So far from greatness consisting in leaving it, it consists in not leaving it." Babbitt, who distrusted "the Jansenist emphasis on thunderclaps and visible upsets of grace," admired the Pascal who differentiated the man of faith from the naturalist, the traditional disciplines from pure naturalism, true faith from "the horrible flux of all things," faith from worldliness. It is the Pascal who finally exclaims, "Joy, certainty, peace," whom Babbitt embraces and whom he equates with the "peace, poise, [and] centrality" he especially admires in Buddhism.

Babbitt's admiration of Pascal shows sympathy not with the ascetical and the mystical, with what he speaks of as the Pascalian "expressions of the theological terror," but rather with the conviction and strength that resist the morbid and discouraging.

"Spiritual strenuousness" remained Babbitt's major tenet of faith: "Work out your own salvation with diligence." Buddha's words dramatize Babbitt's religious orientation, one which clearly disavowed "dogmatic or revealed religion" and the doctrine of grace. G. K. Chesterton, in opposing Superhumanism to Humanism, regarded the latter as one of those "spiritual experiments outside the central spiritual tradition." "Humanism may try to pick up the pieces; but can it stick them together?" Chesterton asks. "Where is the cement which made religion corporate and popular, which can prevent it falling to pieces in a *débris* of individualistic tastes and degrees?"[1]

Babbitt's qualified acceptance of Pascal is indicative of his discernment of institutional religion and its fundamental ideas. His endorsements were selective and limiting. In the religious realm, as in the educational, Babbitt was motivated by a positive critical spirit informed by his absolute rejection of any romantic tendency culminating in man's "expansive conceit" that produces ignorance and blindness. His religious views have a decidedly generalist cast and belong to what should be called the universal moral order. In contemporary religious parlance, Babbitt could be termed an "ecumenist," though this word would be apt to imply nonselective and nondefined religious elements that Babbitt would find antipathetic. Babbitt's religious search goes beyond the frontiers of historical Christianity and is more inclusive in its figures, goals, and essences, as he makes clear when he writes: "...if there is such a thing as the wisdom of the ages, a central core of normal human experience, this wisdom is, on the religious level, found in Buddha and

Christ and, on the humanistic level, in Confucius and Aristotle. These teachers may be regarded both in themselves and in their influence as the four outstanding figures in the spiritual history of mankind."

This statement identifies the comprehensive features of Babbitt's religious quest, even as it points to its heterodox features. Yet to insist on Babbitt's religious deviationism does him a disservice. Any fair consideration of his thought will corroborate Professor Louis J.A. Mercier's contention that, for Babbitt, man is a rational animal in whom there is felt "the presence of a higher will ultimately divine." Indeed, in one of his later essays, "Humanism: An Essay at Definition," Babbitt affirms Pascal's belief that the humanist must finally take part in the debate between naturalists and supernaturalists. Babbitt proceeds to state a principle of belief that elucidates the religious character of his humanism: "For my own part, I range myself unhesitatingly on the side of the supernaturalists. Though I see no evidence that humanism is necessarily ineffective apart from dogmatic and revealed religion, there is, as it seems to me, evidence that it gains immensely in effectiveness when it has a background of religious insight."

In their thrust and ramification Babbitt's religious ideas and acceptances are cautious. Any excess of rarefied religious sentiment or spirituality is checked. One cannot, he iterates, pass from the human to the religious level too quickly; the world would be better if men "made sure that they were human before setting out to be superhuman." There are priorities to be observed, levels of growth to be attained, particular paths to be followed, and adjustments to be made if humanism and religion are to have a gainful encounter. At the same time, Babbitt avers, "humanistic mediation that has the support of meditation may correctly be said to have a religious background. Mediation and meditation are after all only different stages in the same ascending 'path' and should not be arbitrarily separated."

Humanism can work in harmony with religion in opposition to what Babbitt sees as a common foe when he writes: "The chief enemies of the humanist are the pragmatists and other philosophers of the flux who simplify this problem for themselves by dismissing the One, which is a living intuition, as a metaphysical abstraction." "Humanism: An Essay at Definition" occupies a high place in an understanding of Babbitt's religious views. Its chief value is corrective. Babbitt was keenly aware of the misunderstanding and misrepresentation of his attitude toward religion. His statements in this essay have a concentrated purpose, not only in definition but also in clarification. He is painstaking in formulating his religious views. "It is an error to hold that humanism can take the place of religion," he emphasizes. "Religion indeed may more readily dispense with humanism than humanism with religion." Here Babbitt is speaking to critical friends, to the Paul Elmer More who asks in trepidation: "Will not the humanist, unless he adds to his creed the faith and the hope of religion, find himself at the last, despite his protests, dragged back into the camp of the naturalist? If we perish like beasts, shall we not live like beasts?"[12]

These are defiant, even embarrassing, questions which Babbitt answered with the patience and dignity of the great teacher that he was. So much more was demanded of Babbitt than of others, perhaps because he, more than others, meditated on first causes and ultimate ends. If anything, Babbitt's orientation was one of opportunities and strivings. Between humanism and the Christian communions Babbitt sought for a basis of cooperation in a united struggle against "the humanitarian programme." "The weakness of humanitarianism from both the humanistic and the religious point[s] of view," he declared, "is that it holds out the hope of securing certain spiritual benefits ...without any ascent from the naturalistic level." What is constant in Babbitt's religious thought is his stress on man's need for a morality of ascent, the ultimate standard of spiritual effort and life. That man needs to submit his ordinary self to some higher will is, for Babbitt, a central religious tenet. In this submission there reside the elements of awe and humility and the ultimate attainment of peace. It is the ethical dimension of religion that he advances. As he remarks: "The final reply to all the doubts that torment the human heart is not some theory of conduct, however perfect, but the man of character." Though Babbitt repeatedly warns of the perils of intellectual unrestraint, he is critical of the Christian tendency to get rid of the intellect in order to get rid of the pride of the intellect. Unfailingly Babbitt keeps his eye on the universal center, on the middle path. As a true Aristotelian, he writes: "To use the intellect to the utmost and at the same time to kept it in its proper subordinate place is a task that seems thus far to have been beyond the capacity of Occidental man."

Not so much an historical, and sacramental, but a critical Christianity is what Babbitt addresses himself to. What he most sympathizes with in Christianity are its elements of joy and illumination; what he most opposes is a "romantic religiosity" mired in "the web of illusion" and "metaphysical despair." Particularly in the Catholic Church did Babbitt find aspects to admire, or what he singled out as its "discipline and the definite standards that could protect society against the individual." On the other hand, he felt that the Protestant churches were turning more and more to the doctrine of social service and thus were "substituting for the truths of the inner life various causes and movements and reforms and crusades."

For Babbitt there was an overarching religious problem that he saw confronting modern man. It went back to Rousseau. That religious problem, Babbitt said, involves a major judgmental choice "between a dualism that affirms a struggle between good and evil in the heart of the individual and the dualism which, like that of Rousseau, transfers the struggle to society." Insofar as the Rousseauistic attitude has prevailed in the modern world, according to Babbitt, spiritual disorder has become ascendant. He was concerned with an existential as opposed to a theological evil, with those forms of evil that embody an evasion of moral responsibility, so that they result in what he termed spiritual indolence. To resist this form of breakdown he prescribes the humanistic virtues—moderation, common sense, and common decency. He viewed these virtues in the context of "a positive and critical humanism" in which there is an emphasis on the educative function: man "must be trained in the appropriate habits almost from infancy." "We need," he says, "to restore to human nature in some critical and experimental fashion the 'old Adam' that the idealists have been so busy eliminating." As necessary as they are, the theological virtues of faith, hope, and charity are subsequent to the humanistic as an ultimate developmental stage in the morality of ascent and in "the paths of Truth."

It bears repeating that Babbitt's attitude toward revealed religion was essentially one of "suspended judgment." He perceived humanism as a common ground upon which dualists, Christians and non-Christians, could meet. No less than the "humanistic Goethe" (as revealed in the *Conversations* with Eckermann and in the critical judgments uttered in his later years), Babbitt "would have us cease theorizing about the absolute and learn to recognize it in its actual manifestations." Man, Babbitt would say, needs to learn the lessons of renunciation, but the renunciation of temperament and impulses must be "the natural outgrowth of this life and not, as so often in religion, the violent contradiction of it." Of Babbitt, as of Goethe, it could be said that he avoided confusing the planes of being. In the Goethe who expressed the humanistic virtues Babbitt found a mirror of himself that enabled him to trace the anatomy of his own religious identity. What was finally disclosed was Babbitt's stress on what he calls "instinct for a sound spiritual hygiene" and on the need to turn away from grace to works. "The right use of grace and similar doctrines," Babbitt states, "is to make us humble and not to make us morbid or discouraged." Speculations about the "insoluble mysteries" are basically unrewarding; like Goethe, Babbitt refused "to enter into the metaphysical maze of either the dogmatic supernaturalist or the dogmatic naturalist."

For Babbitt, "sham spirituality" signifies the death of faith. Throughout his writings he provides a diagnostic examination of what he judges to be religious illusions and errors emerging from a monistic naturalism. Babbitt locates standards of what he calls "true spirituality," the truths of humility and of the inner life, in the Orient, especially in the religion and personality of Buddha. In Buddhism, Babbitt applauds a comparative freedom from casuistry, obscurantism, and intolerance. The most significant religious statement that Babbitt makes on the subject is his long introductory essay "Buddha and the Occident," found in his translation of the ancient Pāli classic of Buddhist wisdom, *The Dhammapada,* published in 1936. This essay is Babbitt's spiritual testament, his final witness. No understanding of his religious ethos is possible without a judicious estimation of this essay.

A lifelong student of Buddhism, Babbitt was much in sympathy with the Primitive *(Hīnayāna)* Buddhism of Ceylon, Burma, and Siam. Austin Warren believes that Babbitt was in fact a Buddhist and was "motivated...by the desire to restate 'genuine Buddhism' in modern terms, as a religion acceptable to those who, like himself, found metaphysics, theology, and ecclesiasticism harmful rather than salutary to the devout life."[13] And Paul Elmer More simply states as a fact that Babbitt "was much closer to Buddhism than would appear from his public utterances."[14] In an essay-review, "Interpreting India to the West" (1917), Babbitt crystalizes his concept of a Buddhism that may be used to supplement and support our Western wisdom when he writes, or rather testifies, his own faith:

> Buddha deals with the law of control, the special law of human nature, in a spirit as positive and dispassionate as that in which a Newton deals with the law of gravitation. If a man wishes peace and brotherhood, he must pay the price—he must rise above the naturalistic level; and this he can do only by overcoming his moral indolence, only by applying the inner check to temperamental impulse.[15]

The experience of the Far East, Babbitt believed, completes and confirms that of the Occident. "We can scarcely afford to neglect it if we hope to work out a truly ecumenical wisdom to oppose to the sinister one-sidedness of our current naturalism," he observes. The historical Buddha, Babbitt believed, was a "critical and experimental supernaturalist," a dualist and individualist who did not rest his belief on those "tremendous affirmations" of dogmatic and revealed religion that revolved around a personal God and personal immortality. Buddha can be defined as a "religious empiricist" to whom the real meaning of faith is "faith to act." Self-mastery is the most eminent aspect of this faith as meaning and as action, that is, as inner action. "Self is the lord of self. Who else can be the lord?" Buddha declares. "By oneself the evil is done, by oneself one is defiled. Purity and impurity belong to oneself, no one can purify another." What ennobles Buddhism, in Babbitt's eyes, is an emphasis on earnestness and on continual spiritual effort to subordinate the evil forces within one to an indwelling law of righteousness. Babbitt especially endorses the words that Buddha uttered at the end of his life: "Therefore, O Ananda, be ye lamps unto yourselves. Be ye refuges unto yourselves. Look to no outer refuge. Hold fast as a refuge unto the Law *(Dhamma).*"

Buddhism is not a philosophical system but a "path"; one who follows this path ultimately gains insight that is marked by an increasing awareness, which precedes "right meditation" and "is at the opposite pole from the diffuse reverie that has been so encouraged by our modern return to nature." Wisdom is measured by the degree to which man has been awakened from "the dream of sense."

In Buddhism, Babbitt perceived a religion rooted in a "psychology of desire." "Immediate peace," not "immediate pleasure," is for Buddha a paramount goal. This peace is the "rest that comes through striving." It is a calm that is "without the slightest trace of languor," a "meditative tranquillity" that arises when, as Buddha says, one "has reached the other shore in two states (tranquillity and insight)." For Babbitt a saint, whether Buddhist or Christian, "is rightly meditative and in proportion to the rightness of his meditation is the depth of his peace." If Christianity was originally more emotional and nostalgic in temper than Buddhism, Babbitt states, "it is at one in its final emphasis with the older religion. In both faiths this emphasis is on the peace that passeth understanding." If, as Babbitt noted, Buddha was filled with pity, he was also very stern; in Buddha, as in Christ, love and justice are perfectly balanced so as to constitute a single virtue. The Buddhist's insistence on self-love may appear to be selfish and uncharitable, but Babbitt went on to stipulate that the teaching of true self-love accentuates the love of a higher self. This Buddhist teaching, he pointed out, is similar to the Christian concept of dying that one may live. He most admired in Buddha the importance given to the role of the intellect that is keenly discriminating and that of the higher will that is strenuous.

The security and the serenity that are at the heart of "religious comfort" have given way, Babbitt lamented, to an obsessive search for material comfort. In this shifting of emphasis he viewed the glorification of the utilitarian and sentimental facets of the humanitarian movement. Basic religious precepts are radically altered so as to satisfy this process of ethical and spiritual transvaluation. "A great religion is above all a great example," Babbitt declares; but "the example tends to grow faint in time or even to suffer alteration into something very different." More than other religious teachers, Buddha, who stands for the idea of meditation, has deep significance for the Occident. This significance is heightened by the fact that Buddha reduces the human problem to a psychology of desire and then deals with desire in terms of conflict and adjustment. Particularly in the passage from the medieval to the modern period, Babbitt contended, the idea of meditation and the transcendent view of life have steadily declined. "Yet it is not certain," Babbitt adds, "that religion itself can survive unless men retain some sense of the wisdom that may, according to Dante, be won by sitting in quiet recollection."

In Buddhism, as tested by its fruits, Babbitt saw a striking confirmation of Christianity. Buddha provides spiritual paradigms and humanistic truths that, if accepted, would augment the Christian faith by saving it, as Babbitt hoped, from a Calvinist nightmare or an Arcadian dream. Buddha's relevance to Christianity, he says, is positive and critical in the sense of reinforcing and remobilizing the intrinsic strength in a modern world. These final sentences from Babbitt's essay "Buddha and the Occident" identify the connections that he sought to establish between two great religious movements in a period that has seen the eclipse of the religious sense:

> The meditation of the Buddhist involves like that of the Christian the exercise of transcendent will; this will is not, however, associated, as it normally is in the meditation of the Christian, with that of a personal deity. Persons of positive and critical temper who yet perceive

the importance of meditation may incline here as elsewhere to put less emphasis on the doctrinal divergence
of Christianity and Buddhism than on their psychological agreement.

Predictably, Babbitt's Christian Platonist friend, Paul
Elmer More, and his Anglo-Catholic pupil, T. S. Eliot, had
other views of Buddhism. Of the two, More's response to
Buddhism was more sympathetic. Unlike Babbitt, More
favored Hindu mysticism and the Brahmanic theosophy of
the *Upanishads.* By the end of his life he had accepted
Christianity as the complement and climax of the Greek
tradition. The first essay in his book *The Catholic Faith* is
devoted to "Buddhism and Christianity"; Babbitt himself
had gone through the entire book with such "extreme
care" as to prompt an extensive revision of that essay. In
ways that recall Babbitt, More brought Buddhism into vital
relation to Christianity; he saw both religions covering and
dividing "the deeper possibilities of faith." In the history of
the two religions he found similarities, as he also found in
the morality of discipline taught by Buddha and by Christ.
More's admiration of the Buddhist's three stages of
progress in sanctity—discipline of conduct, discipline of
mind, and the higher wisdom and power—is no less than
Babbitt's.

But More discerned profound absences in Buddhism: it
contains no Creator, no providential Ruler, no Judge, no
Savior. Like Babbitt, he considered Buddhism more joyous
and even-tempered than Christianity, but, in contrast to
the latter, More believed that "the notion of *telos* plays no
part in its cosmogony or ethics." That is, in Buddhism there
is "no continuity between the end and the means to the
end." Though More admitted that Buddha was "the noblest
of all religious teachers, saving only one," and that
Buddhism, by its reticence about the soul and by its very
omission of God, "was preserved from the evils of intoler-

ance and fanaticism and spiritual anguish that have so often darkened the history of Christianity," he also stressed that Buddhism has "missed something of the positive riches of experience that Christianity at its best can bestow." In what can be construed as a magnanimous rebuttal of Babbitt's position, More concludes with these words regarding Buddha:

> ...it seems to me at times as if that great soul were searching on all the ways of the spirit for the dogma of the Incarnation, and that fact of the historic Jesus, could it have been known to him, might have saved his religion in later ages from floundering helplessly.... Buddhism, I think, may be accepted as a preface to the Gospel...and as the most convincing argument withal that truth to be clearly known waits upon revelation.

Far less magnanimous is Eliot's critique of Babbitt's Buddhism. It leaves the distinct impression that Eliot, once and for all, is dismissing a heretic who dismisses the doctrine of revelation. This critique constitutes a long introductory essay written by Eliot for a collection entitled *Revelation,* edited by John Baillie and Hugh Martin, and published in 1937. Eliot categorically declares that "the division between those who accept, and those who deny, Christian revelation I take to be the most profound division between human beings." Throughout, his critical perspective is tough and unsparing. In Babbitt he sees "the most remarkable, the most ambitious attempt to erect a secular philosophy of life in our time." He terms Babbitt a "disbeliever," unique because "he attacked the foundations of secularism more deeply and more comprehensively than any other writer of our time."

Eliot concentrates on the essay "Buddha and the Occident" in order to show how Babbitt sought "to evade Christian conclusions at any cost." The Buddhism of

Babbitt, he concludes, instances a kind of "psychological mysticism." "This is the mysticism which seeks contact with the sources of supernatural power," writes Eliot, "divorced from religion and theology; the mysticism which must always be suspect, and which sometimes springs up in cults whose aims are not far removed from those of magic." Especially interesting in Eliot's essay is his coupling of Babbitt and D. H. Lawrence: "The point is that the will to get out from Christianity into a religion of one's own operated in Lawrence as it operated in Babbitt." Eliot ends his discussion of "the literature of secularism" by remarking that the religious sentiment, which can be satisfied only by the message of revelation, "is simply suffering from a condition of repression painful for those in whom it is repressed, who yearn for the fulfillment of belief, although too ashamed of that yearning to allow it to come to consciousness."

That Eliot is doubtlessly aware of his arbitrary yoking of Babbitt and Lawrence in their "will against Christianity" is suggested by the tone in which he distinguishes Babbitt ("by nature an educated man, as well as a highly well-informed one") from Lawrence ("a medicine man" and "a researcher into religious emotion"). But his indictment of both men as examples of "individualistic misdirections of will" is uncompromising insofar as both men, he claims, teach and affirm secular philosophies and are examples of "titanism," "the attempt to build a purely human world without reliance upon grace."

Eliot's case against Lawrence's "religion of power and magic" has been largely answered by F. R. Leavis. The case against Babbitt, however, remains curiously unanswered, perhaps because of the paradoxical alliance between Babbitt's Christian friends and his liberal enemies, who propagate Eliot's thesis for their special purposes. The fact remains that Babbitt's humanist beliefs cannot be understood without the background of his religious thinking.

He was not an orthodox Christian, but he gave his spiritual witness in the very character of his writing and teaching. He had integrity. He had humility, the humility that Eliot tells us is endless. And he had standards. These qualities never failed to compass his work and thought: his judgments, which he conveyed resolutely and directly. "There appears to be evidence," he says, "that religion has existed without the accompaniment of morality." Such a statement again reminds us that, for Babbitt, the validity of religion lies in psychology rather than in history, and makes even more emphatic Babbitt's reverence for the Buddha who declares in his message of joyful deliverance: "Only one thing I announce today, as always, Sorrow and its Extinction."

To connect and unify the inner life and the outer life constituted for Babbitt a paramount spiritual need. Those who face up to the moral requisites of this need, he believed, "face unflinchingly the facts of life and these facts do not encourage a thoughtless elation." Thus Babbitt esteemed Saint Francis de Sales because this Doctor of the Church had worked out a synthesis between the demands of "this-worldliness" and those of "other-worldliness." By the same token, Babbitt frowned upon Byzantine sacred art, obviously detecting in the ikons of the Eastern Church an obscure, even passive, soteriological quality that he equated with excessive melancholy and with the loss of "one's self in a shoreless sea of reverie."

In respect to sacred music, too, Babbitt had clear-cut views. He stressed the need to distinguish between the genuine "devotional music" of Christian plainsong, which inspires prayer and peace, and the "insurrectional music" of *The Requiem Mass* of Hector Berlioz, which Babbitt equated with "emotional unrestraint" and with sheer "noise and sensationalism." Spiritual romanticism, for Babbitt, was no less harmful than the romanticism that subverts the aesthetic criteria of "dignity, centrality, repose." In particular he distrusted what he termed "the expansion of infinite indeterminate desire" that he related to the neo-Platonic side of Christianity, though he was careful to praise that aspect of the Christian faith that "has dealt sternly and veraciously with the facts of human nature. It has perceived clearly how a man may move towards happiness and how on the other hand he tends to sink into despair; or what amounts to the same thing, it has seen the supreme importance of spiritual effort and the supreme danger of spiritual sloth." It is almost unnecessary to theorize how Babbitt would view the current vogue of "liberation theology," which revolves so loosely and sentimentally around a messianic materialism and the whirl of "the secular city." Such a theology of unilateral desanctification, Babbitt would say, is another blatant example of "eleutheromania."

We must not judge Babbitt according to a systematic or dogmatic theology; his was not a concern with what Paul Tillich designates as the theology that "is the methodical explanation of the contents of the Christian faith." First and last Babbitt was a moral critic and comparatist, who saw "connections that no other mind would have perceived," as Eliot wrote of his "old teacher and master." Babbitt practiced the wisdom of Confucius' admonition that "the man who does not take far views will have near troubles." On the first page of *Democracy and Leadership* he writes: "When studied with any degree of thoroughness, the economic problem will be found to run into the political problem, the political problem in turn into the philosophical problem, and the philosophical problem itself to be almost indissolubly bound up at last with the religious problem." These noble words help to identify Babbitt's achievement in its value and "constant aspiration toward the central unity of life." Nor must we forget that he was a teacher, a *didaskalos,* "an enlightener and enlarger." Hence to assess his religious significance in terms of a theological orthodoxy is to violate the intrinsic spiritual strength of his thought. He was not a religionist, nor a philosopher of religion, nor a teacher of theology. He was quintessentially a spiritual man, indeed, a spiritual genius, "to whom reality was the spiritual life," to recall Warren's words. He revered the interior life, as well as the ethical and moral life. He possessed an informing religious sense, not one that was vague and numinous, but analytical and judgmental. He sought for a "sense of the absolute," for the absolute of an Emerson or a Tennyson, which Babbitt defined as "a purely spiritual perception of the light beyond reason, entirely disassociated from the faith in creeds and formulas."

There is some truth in R. P. Blackmur's symptomatic complaint that Babbitt was a preacher,[16] if by preacher one means a humanistic and religious realist who traces causes and effects and who distinguishes between the law of the spirit and the law of the members, between the "law for man" and the "law for thing." Such a realist finds a common good in morality and affirms the meaning of the moral real and the meaning of all existence within the universal moral real. The religious sense diminishes, as Babbitt averred, when moral struggle and deliberation and choice are minimized. He vividly imaged this reductionist process in his contrast "between the spiritual athlete and the cosmic loafer, between a Saint Paul...and a Walt Whitman." "The greater a man's moral seriousness," he reminds us, "the more he will be concerned with doing rather than dreaming." Babbitt clearly indicated that he had no aversion to a humanist who, seeking support in something higher than reason, turns to Christian theology. "I hold that at the heart of genuine Christianity," he declares, "are certain truths which have already once saved Western civilization and, judiciously employed, may save it again." But he also claimed that for one to be fully positive and critical in the modern world, one has to deal with life more psychologically than metaphysically. He thought it possible, perhaps necessary, to conceive of a humanistic or even a religious psychology that transcends both the dictates of a naturalistic psychology and the symbolic view of the world.

Indeed, Babbitt saw a close affinity between the elimination of the teleological element from modern life and the decline of traditional religion and the older religious controls. He nevertheless believed that, from a humanistic point of view, to restore this teleological element it is more advantageous to start with psychological observation, as in early Buddhism, rather than with theological affirmations. Warning against "dogmatic exclusiveness," he says that one could eclectically acquire humanistic and religious purpose without indulging in ultimates and absolutes. "The good life," he writes, "is not primarily something to be known but something to be willed." And when "willed" the life-problem of avoiding the "indolence of extremes" is mitigated.

Irving Babbitt chose to speak out not as an orthodox Christian but simply as "a psychological observer" and a "complete positivist." In this capacity he judged "the modern movement," the social benefits of which he found largely illusory and the spiritual offshoots of which made "neither for humanistic poise nor again for the peace of religion." He discriminated practically and concretely between true and false religion. His standards were clear and unshakable in demarcating and avoiding "a confusion of categories." Any softening of standards, he never ceased to state, has a commensurate impact on spiritual life. A dire threat to religious, and humanistic, standards, Babbitt said, is man's consuming "interest in origins rather than in ends." In this connection, he especially esteemed Aristotle's dictum, "the first thing is not seed but the perfect being."[17] These words, it should be remembered, closely follow Aristotle's other emphatic declaration, in his *Metaphysics,* that "life belongs to God." The critical centrality of his religious views must be fully comprehended if Babbitt's moral and spiritual vision is to be saved from both the tests of religious orthodoxy and the incubus of heresy. When this reparative task has been finally accomplished, then what Boswell said of Dr. Johnson will be said of Babbitt—that he is, incontestably, a "majestic teacher of moral and religious wisdom."

## CHAPTER FOUR

# Irving Babbitt
# and Simone Weil

## I

The abridgement of the heroic spirit is as common to the modern age as is what Thomas Hardy called "the abridgement of hope." We live in a world in which exhaustion is the most unconditional human condition. We have fallen so deep into a collective crisis-situation that human destiny is no longer regarded with fear and trembling. Our moral confusion transposes into moral desuetude. That prophecy of despair announced in the concluding section of Dostoevsky's *Crime and Punishment* (1866) becomes increasingly a bleak reality of world-fact. That apocalypse of the abyss, as warned steadily by existentialists since the "Armistice" of 1918, seems irreversible. The disappearance, the eclipse, the death of God, as variously described, reveal a waste land in its inner depths and outer reaches. It is hardly necessary even to remark on the moribundity of the Judaeo-Christian concepts of man and the universe. Post-historical man has reached an impasse. Indeed, is it possible that, with the demise of Kafka's Joseph K., murdered "like a dog," the humanistic world hears its death-knell? But this song of lamentation needs no further, oppressive elaboration. T. S. Eliot captures the modern predicament in words that return us to lost beginnings and broken endings when he writes:

> Son of man,
> You cannot say, or guess, for you know only
> A heap of broken images, where the sun beats,
> And the dead tree gives no shelter,
> the cricket no relief,
> And the dry stone no sound of water.

Eliot reminds us of poets as prophets contemplating the human scene. We are also reminded that, whatever the extent and depth of man's failure of nerve or his spiritual homelessness, the creative impulse and the heroic spirit can advance in a reciprocal visionary process, manifesting the modern equivalent of a miracle and a mystery. D. H. Lawrence captures the life-saving quality of this process when he declares: "Brave men [and women] are for ever born, and nothing else is worth having." As long as each of us can point to the enduring worth of Lawrence's words by being able to designate its particular exemplars—whether as great poets or novelists, or as great critics or teachers— then what appears as futile in the changing aspects of the historical situation is not final. Belief in the life of value has continuing worth. The creative principle redeems human possibility. We are not as fully defeated as Samuel Beckett would have us think when he points to "the absolute absence of the absolute."

That we do possess first principles; that we can locate a center of values, however frightening modern man's inner and outer turmoil and the cruel swiftness of changes wrought by an even crueller history: it is in the insistence on these axiomatic truths that Irving Babbitt, who died in 1933, and Simone Weil, who died ten years later, come together as teachers and critics exemplifying the meaning of Lawrence's statement. Ultimately, too, their critical comparability has a spiritual element that helps to relate the American-Aristotelian New Humanist and the French-Jewish Christian Platonist.

Both viewed with alarm the rise of the naturalistic and relativistic ethos of the modern age. Both were engaged in resisting what Simone Weil saw as the menace of the "Great Beast" of atheism, materialism, and totalitarianism. Both were preoccupied with the eternal struggle between good and evil in the individuating contexts of what Simone Weil imaged as "gravity and grace" and of what Babbitt tested in the categorizing terms of two discrete and irreconcilable laws, the law for man and the law for thing. Both insisted on the ethical, moral character of ascendance and on recalling the ever-informing substance of the venerable words, in their intrinsic contrasts of value, that our "sociological dreamers and reformers," as Babbitt called them, have debased: virtue, nobility, honor, honesty, generosity, decorum, reverence, discipline. Both were profoundly concerned with the spiritual idea of value and, consequently, with the burden of moral responsibility. Both stressed the necessity for the defining discernment of standards on all levels of life and specifically that operative standard which revolves around some absolute spiritual principle of unity measuring mere manifoldness and change. Babbitt chose to connect this standard of standards with what he conceived of as "the wisdom of the ages." Simone Weil was no less adamant in her view of an absolute criterion of transcendence, that which embodies "submission of those parts which have had no contact with God to the one which has."

The critical affinities between Irving Babbitt and Simone Weil go much deeper than their grounding in the French literary thought of the seventeenth century, or in their reverence for the classical tradition, or in their admiration of Oriental religious and philosophical thought. One must see them as critics scrupulously examining what

Babbitt indicted as "the progressive decline of standards" and the "inordinate self-confidence of modern man." Their critiques of society are both diagnostic and prescriptive, particularly aiming to warn man not to give his first and final allegiance to the god of Whirl, nor to the religion of a cheap contemporaneousness, with its lusts for sensation, knowledge, and power, and with its new gospel that, in Simone Weil's words, asserts that "matter is a machine for manufacturing the good."

As critics of their time, which remains our own in its steady rhythm of disintegration, they saw their roles in the implicitly moral terms of a critical mission. Each accepted the painful consequences that are a part of any mission that taunts man with the message that in perilous times he has an even more perilous need of moral transcendence and transfiguration. Each undertook a role that was supremely critical, didactic, and moral. Each demanded, and expected, of his contemporaries perhaps more than they were willing or able to give. A spiritual renovation of mankind or a renewal of individual man is often better arranged in theoretical contexts than in actual and discriminating fact. Babbitt undoubtedly had this in mind when he said that modern man's chief need was to be not less but more positive and critical in scrutinizing life-experience and life-value. Even to ask the right questions, he said, is no small distinction. Babbitt's words, as they portend moral action, help us to recall these words of Simone Weil: "If, as is only too possible, we are to perish, let us see to it that we do not perish without having existed."

What preeminently connects Irving Babbitt and Simone Weil in their view of the world is an unceasing concern with the meaning of man and with the destiny of mankind. The ultimate question of evil is for both inescapable. To seek to avoid confronting "the wickedness of human nature," as Aristotle puts it, constitutes a betrayal of man's moral responsibility. It is a decision to remain, as

Simone Weil would sum it up, in a state of physical gravity, which pulls us away from God and makes us captives of the outer life with all its false idols. The struggle between good and evil is a constant of human existence, or as Babbitt expresses it: "Poets and reformers need not waste time speculating about the *origin* of evil, but they surely cannot be blind to the *fact* of evil." No less hesitantly Simone Weil avers, concerning the "civil war in the cave," that "we cannot contemplate without terror the extent of the evil which man can do and endure."

Man's encounter with evil demands careful discrimination between moral progress and material progress. For Babbitt this discrimination specially compels vigilance against "the temperamental view of life." The life of value is tied to the required standard of vital, of ethical and rational, control. It culminates in "a rest that comes through striving." "Men cannot come together in a common sympathy," he insists, "but only in a common discipline." To be sure, Babbitt's attitude towards evil was moral and humanistic, whereas Simone Weil's was moral and sacramental. Babbitt's attitude belongs to the category of religious empiricism, Simone Weil's to that of religious mysticism. The difference is obviously crucial. Babbitt believed in the imperative of moral discipline, which he saw as a defense against the dominance over modern man being steadily exerted by the power-centers of utilitarianism, empiricism, positivism, and liberalism. Evil not only can be detected but also must be faced in the maleficent shifting of standards, in the inclination, as Babbitt phrased it, "to eliminate the will to refrain and the inner effort it involves in favor of a mere outer working."

It is true that Simone Weil believed that life is filled with impossibility and absurdity and that man must aim for a higher purifying process of "decreation," of disincarnation. But it is also essential to recognize her firm grasp of social reality and necessity. "The world is the closed door.

It is a barrier. And at the same time it is the way through," she maintains. Her reflections on and insights into social reality and necessity are as rigorous and unsentimental, as concentrated and analytical as any of Irving Babbitt's. To view Simone Weil as one curiously suffering from the vertigo of the absolute is to misunderstand and misrepresent her intuitive awareness of the ever destructive mechanisms of what she calls "the empire of might." Nothing better illustrates the depth of her view of a social order in disequilibrium, nor, indeed, better relates Irving Babbitt and Simone Weil as critics of modern society, than these words from her essay "Reflections on Quantum Theory":

> Everything is oriented towards utility, which nobody thinks of defining: public opinion reigns supreme, in the village of scientists as in the great nations. It is as though we had returned to the age of Protagoras and the Sophists, the age when the art of persuasion—whose modern equivalent is advertising slogans, publicity, propaganda meetings, the press, the cinema, and radio—took the place of thought and controlled the fate of cities and accomplished *coups d'état*.

Neither Babbitt's nor Simone Weil's social-political judgments have as yet found an audience. Today, as in the 1920s and 1930s, it remains fashionable to dismiss Babbitt's views as a mere sanction of New England and Republican prejudices. Simone Weil has not fared much better. Even if her life has intrigued the American intelligentsia, her religious and philosophical thought is often bifurcated or else subordinated to what critics label the "passions of the 'Red Virgin' " or "the mystery of Simone Weil"—the "passions" and "mystery" here undoubtedly connoting neuroticism or anomaly. Babbitt continues to be dogged by the nemesis of Edmund Wilson's celebrated, and calculated, remark that "the writings of the humanist[s] strike us with a chill even more mortal than that of reason." Simone Weil's nemesis has a more seignorial authority of tone and rejection in the person of none other than General Charles de Gaulle: "She's out of her mind," he said. Today's literary politicians of revolution reject Babbitt's critical achievement as the epitome of the "administrative" attitude toward life and thought. The continuing endorsement of the abusers of Babbitt's thought is, at the very least, symptomatic of the breakdown of standards in our civilization, the causes of which Babbitt himself mercilessly delineated. Reaction to Simone Weil's social and political writings underlines a now all-too-predictable conditioned reflex: they are condescendingly associated with her primarily spiritual message, and anything that is tinged with the word "spirit" is immediately suspect and expendable. "Dean Inge, one fancies, would approve of her metaphysics"—so we are told, the words, in tone and accent, containing a blanket reduction of Simone Weil's significance as a thinker whose belief in "the need for roots" presupposes exacting moral standards.

## II

Not prophets of salvation, but prophets of utopian revolution (and resexualization), with their promises of an ecstatic entrance through the "gates of Eden," are today our real cultural heroes. The criteria of wisdom and the paths of meditation implicit in the sapiential criticism of Babbitt and Simone Weil are what the "imperial self" of our technologico-Benthamite society treats as luxury or nonsense. "The belief in moral responsibility," Babbitt declares, "must be based on a belief in the possibility of an inner working of some kind with reference to standards. The utilitarian...has put his main emphasis on outer working. The consequence of this emphasis, coinciding as it has with the multiplication of machines, has been the substitution of standardization for standards." Babbitt's words, or better his demand for moral austerity and intellectual seriousness, help to explain why he is the enemy in the eyes of those "geometricians in regard to matter" (to use Simone Weil's phrase), who, following a John Dewey or a Herbert Marcuse, promulgate the tenets of "organized intelligence," of "scientific method," of "technological application." It is precisely in their opposition to the modern theories of evolutionism, progressivism, and material secularism, in their uncompromising commitment to the "permanent things," and, hence, in their quest for a basic spiritual orientation in the human realm, that Babbitt and Simone Weil become allies. Such an alliance, always vulnerable despite its possession of the assurance of first principles, must inevitably confront the collected power of a solipsistic titanism, in short, that "permanent force of the world," to quote Eliot, "against which the spirit must always struggle."

Nowhere is this collision better seen than in two books that confront the permanent power of the world and that illuminate the human corollaries and moral consequences of such a struggle, Babbitt's *Democracy and Leadership* (1924) and Simone Weil's *The Need for Roots* (1949). Both books belong to what Eliot calls "that prolegomena to politics which politicians seldom read, and which most of them would be unlikely to understand or to know how to apply."

*Democracy and Leadership* is perhaps Babbitt's most vigorous, completing, and configurating synthesis of his thought; its dialectical integrity and relevance are incontrovertible. It asks fundamental questions that remain peculiarly unanswered by our "cosmic loafers," as he dubbed them. And it contains an unflinching indictment of the Baconian, Rousseauistic, and Machiavellian, that is the utilitarian, sentimental, and imperialistic, doctrines that have contributed to the most nagging modern problem— the absence of leaders with standards. The consequences and concomitants of this absence, he stresses, are disastrously identifiable in the drifting that characterizes ethics and politics; in the softness that is not civilization; in the expansive emotion that does not constitute the inner life. And what, in effect, is even worse than a resultant lack of vision is the prevalence of "sham vision"; pinpointing what remains one of the most shocking sanctimonies of our narcissist society, Babbitt observes: "Otherwise stated, what is disquieting about the time is not so much its open and avowed materialism as what it takes to be its spirituality." We have here a prophetic truth, the continuing applicability of which our contemporary "apostles of modernity," ever zealous in attaining the final "demystification of authority," would be pleased not to deny.

In *Democracy and Leadership* he pays close attention to what he calls "imperialism" not only in the social-political but also in the psychological sense. In this imperialism he sees man's centrifugal push for more power, whether in terms of Machiavelli's political naturalism, or of Hobbes's violent materialism, or of Bergson's creative evolutionism. The clear and present dangers of such a push—reliance on naked force, disregard of humility and wisdom, absence of inner discipline and of reverence for some ethical center or principle of oneness—stress for Babbitt the crisis of leadership and the impasse of democracy. Rousseau's "idyllic imagination," rather than Burke's "moral imagination," dictates the expansionist tendencies of modern society, and the law of the average becomes the divinity of the average. "One should...in the interests of democracy itself," Babbitt advises, "seek to substitute the doctrine of the right man for the doctrine of the rights of man."

Babbitt's diagnostic judgment concerning the very nature of leadership is undeniable: Lawmakers who themselves have no standards can hardly impose standards on others. If for Babbitt there is a greater moral awareness to be gained from the "immediate data of consciousness," for others any intrinsic awareness that "life is an act of faith" has signified "nothing but negative behavior." Babbitt, we hear R. P. Blackmur grumbling, "struck down too much for discrimination, and he ignored too much for judgment." It is almost unnecessary to comment on the perverseness of this statement except to say that, for too long, it has gone unchallenged.

Simone Weil in *The Need for Roots* lays bare the foundations of modern secularism. No less than Babbitt, she believes that there can be neither the assigning of values except in terms of ends, nor a discovery of universal ultimate values except in terms of universal ultimate ends. And no less than Babbitt she insists that "of all the needs of the soul none is more vital than the Past,"—that Past which is the image "of eternal supernatural reality." Simone Weil completed *The Need for Roots* shortly before her death in 1943, while she was working for the Free French in London. Though conceived as a manual for the post-war renovation of France, it is concerned with the fate of Western society and specifically with the most pronounced sickness of that society: uprootedness, or deracination. Her most mature synthesis of her social-political and religious views, *The Need for Roots* singles out four obstacles separating modern man from a form of civilization that has organic worth: the false conception of greatness; the degradation of the sentiment of justice; the idolization of money; and the lack of religious inspiration. Above all it indicts the theory of evolutionism and the philosophy of progressivism, denouncing, on the one hand, the materialistic conception of a present that moves into the future and, on the other hand, affirming man's moral destiny as a transit from time into eternity. "Progress toward a lesser imperfection," she declares, "is not produced by the desire for a lesser imperfection. Only the desire for perfection has the virtue of being able to destroy in the soul some part of the evil that defiles it."

*The Need for Roots* proposes a code of obligations. In the very first sentence, we read: "The notion of obligations comes before that of rights, which is subordinate and relative to the former." These obligations, she shows, remain independent of conditions, transcend the world, are eternal insofar as they are co-extensive with the eternal destiny of human beings. The list of obligations towards human beings as such corresponds to the list of human needs analogous to hunger. The soul, like the body, has needs that, when lacking, leave it in a famished state. Among these needs Simone Weil lists Order as the first, noting that in modern life, especially since 1789, incompatibility exists between obligations. She writes: "Whoever acts in such a way as to diminish it is an agent of order. Whoever, so as to simplify problems, denies the existence of certain obligations has, in his heart, made a compact with crime." Among other needs of the soul she includes Duty, Obedience, Honor, and Hierarchy (that is, "the scale of responsibilities").

One must not theorize that in her social-political views Simone Weil falls into a compassion that turns into "murderous pity." No one is more aware that "force is sovereign here below" or that barbarism is a permanent and universal phenomenon: "We are [she states] always barbarous towards the weak unless we make an effort of generosity which is as rare as genius." A study not only of *The Need for Roots* but of her earlier social-political essays collected in the volume entitled *Oppression and Liberty* (1958), as well as of her most famous essay, the first to appear in English, "*The Iliad,* Poem of Might" (1940, 1941), will confirm the depth of her attempt "to discredit empty abstractions and analyse concrete problems...in every domain of political and social life." The thrust of her thought is contained in the last complete paragraph that she ever wrote, found in her essay "Is There a Marxist Doctrine?" There she applauds Marx's deep concern for human misery and his conjoining belief that weakness can be a social mechanism for "producing paradise." Yet she also sees the final absurdity of his position when she writes: "Marx accepted this contradiction of strength in weakness, without accepting the supernatural which alone renders the contradiction valid."

Politically, Irving Babbitt and Simone Weil are obviously not in vogue, and their political views are dismissed as being conservative and illiberal. Babbitt is written off as a fascist. Simone Weil is categorized as a non-political and even an anti-political eccentric. The liberal intellectual establishment promotes and maintains this political ostracism. Any serious thinker who reminds us of moral obligations and duties is seen as a threat to the secular city of the world. Any doctrine with rooted metaphysical principles pre-dating Marx's dialectical materialism or Freud's sexual materialism is scorned as antediluvian. Any emphasis on humanistic or on religious discipline, and particularly as this discipline condemns the proliferating obscenities of the contemporary life-style, is derided. The ideas of Irving Babbitt and of Simone Weil, hence, insofar as they present a potential threat to a reigning orthodoxy of enlightenment, are downgraded at every opportunity. Their insistence on the idea of human limitation is, in the end, what both brings them together and what also ignites the most hostile opposition. For Babbitt this emphasis on limitation, and on what he called "the inner check," revolves around his profound suspicion of the impulses of expansionism that create the Rousseauistic illusion of unchecked progress and perfectibility in the human realm. Ultimately, he believes, this makes for arrogance at every level of human thought and activity. For Simone Weil this emphasis on limitation revolves around her indictment of a secular, materialistic ethos that abrogates the idea of the Divine. Only God, she maintains, is perfect and it is for man to pursue the higher spiritual forms of perfection. Babbitt and Simone Weil affirm a priority and a standard of belief, a transcendent moral purpose, hard and uncompromising, that tests social and political life in the contexts of "permanent things."

Essentially, their political views are absolutist in the best and highest sense of the word. That is, the politics of each is rooted in metaphysical criteria, in ultimates that transcend the immediate and the expedient, the relativistic, the empirical. Babbitt's constitutes a politics of ethical vision. He demands strict adherence to a value-system informed by scrupulosity and insistent on an ongoing moral effort that challenges naturalism, impressionism, subjectivism, experimentation: in short that which resists the centrifugal constituents of modern political liberalism. His political attitude is, in this respect, old-fashioned and simple insofar as, first, last, and always, he views the value of all political thought in direct proportion to its adequacy in dealing with the problem of leadership. Political thought and political action must be judged in their inextricability. At the center of each there is to be identified either a positive, virtuous force or a negative, evil one. In this belief Babbitt sought to embrace and maintain a concentric standard of political thought and action. Politics was for him not so much a euphemistic art of the possible but rather a practicing discipline centered in the power of discriminating. In the political realm standards of discrimination attained their beginnings and their endings, as well as their definition and their universality, in unconditional moral contexts.

Babbitt's political emphasis is on an individual and not on a collective orientation. Politics cannot be absolved from the truths of the inner life. A political orientation that emerges through the abstraction from moral distinctions, Babbitt never tires of stressing, must lead to moral obtuseness on all levels of thought and action. It leads, that is, to an orientation, in reality a disorientation, that negates the causal nexus. For Babbitt a positive political orientation is one that affirms an abiding unity; a negative political orientation asserts flux and relativity. The politics of naturalism is perhaps another way of depicting this latter process. Babbitt could neither accept nor endorse the opinion of so many modern political theorists that since there are no permanent problems there are also no permanent alternatives. He judged the political realm, as he did the entire human realm, in relation to the opposition it offers between the principle of control and the expansive desires. The political problem which he confronted, and which he saw as the most serious confronting modern man, was one that he associated with the phenomenon of material efficiency concomitant with ethical inefficiency. In his view of modern politics Babbitt never failed to see and make connections, to take, in short, the far view.

Simone Weil's judgmental response to social organization is always that of a political moralist; she is particularly severe in her rejection of the uncritically accepted myth of revolution and of material progress. Inevitably she casts a cold eye not only on the mechanics of society but also on the exercise of political power, as one can see, respectively, in those two interrelated political tracts that, in their sustained development, meaning, and wholeness, have earned her a permanent place of importance among political theorists: "Reflections Concerning the Causes of Liberty and Social Oppression" (1934), the long essay now included in *Oppression and Liberty*, and *The Need for Roots*. (She considered her long essay as her "testament"; Albert Camus, who later served as a devoted editor of her posthumous works, praised it as being unequaled, since Marx's writings, in its social, political, and economic insights.)

In both these tracts the approach, the tone, the criteria of judgment disclose an impelling austerity and honesty—a critical disinterestedness "of the first magnitude," as Alain, Simone Weil's famous teacher, said—that are, in fact, crystallized in Spinoza's words of advice to a philosopher that she quotes as an epigraph to "Reflections Concerning the Causes of Liberty and Social Oppression": "With regard to human affairs, not to laugh, not to cry, not to become indignant, but to understand." With special reference to Marx, who, she felt, "arrived at a morality which placed the social category to which he belonged—that of professional revolutionaries—above sin," she goes on to stress that the phenomenon of revolution, like the phenomenon of power, is generally destructive. The former, emancipating not men but productive forces (as in Soviet Russia), leads to a "religion of productive forces." And the latter phenomenon ultimately signals "the race for power [that] enslaves everybody, strong and weak alike." Together these two phenomena create "the mechanism of oppression," one of the primary and ineradicable "conditions of existence."

Simone Weil saw the social machine as leading to greater centralization and ultimately to a "blind collectivity." She especially decried the paradox of the process by which judgment of values is increasingly entrusted to material objects, to the power-machine. For within the automatisms of the social-political process she saw the invasion of modern civilization by an ever-increasing disorder. And for her this contributed to a "destructive disequilibrium." Her social and moral sensitivity was, in these crucial matters, particularly keen: "Human existence is so fragile a thing and exposed to such dangers that I cannot love without trembling." Modern technological society, she contends, accepts material progress too easily and complacently, ignoring the conditions at the cost of which it occurs.

Her assessment of the whole of modern thought, since the Renaissance, is tough and unsentimental in exposing what she terms "vague aspirations towards a utopian civilization." Diagnostic insight characterizes her penetration into what has become increasingly the thought—the great liberal illusion—behind the belief in the triumph of mechanisms of matter. This belief, she insists, reduces life to mere instrumentality. Now, as we are nearing the end of the second millennium, what Simone Weil says in the following words has a validity that is incontrovertible in its relevance of meaning as a counter-prophecy to Marx's millennial vision: "The very being of man is nothing else but a perpetual straining after an unknown good. And the materialist is a man. That is why he cannot prevent himself from ultimately regarding matter as a machine for manufacturing the good."

## III

It will be said that Babbitt would have disapproved of Simone Weil on the same intellectual basis that he disapproved of "the tremendous spiritual romanticism" of Saint Augustine. It will be said also that he would have been sharply critical of the mystical essence of her thought, viewing it as an excess of "metaphysical illusion" or a form of postponement and procrastination. Her eschatological concepts of "gravity and grace," of "waiting for God," of "the love of God and affliction" would have seemed unduly ascetical, even morbid, to one who believed in the complete moral responsibility and effort of the individual. Undoubtedly, too, in some aspects of her life he would have detected signs of effusive self-expression—her early left-wing activities like picketing and refusing to eat more than did French workers on relief; her experiences as a factory worker and as a farmhand; her brief service as a member of an anarchist training unit in the Spanish Civil War.

For Babbitt, in whom, as Paul Elmer More remarked, "the immobility of his central ideas" was a monolithic characteristic, Simone Weil would have revealed a mode of sensibility that tended to separate his humanism as much from her Platonic sensibility as from emotional romanticism. Even in their study of Oriental religious thought their antithetical preferences are telling: Babbitt preferred the Pāli language and the Buddhist sacred texts stressing adherence to the laws.

Simone Weil preferred the Sanskrit language and the *Upanishads,* with their speculative and mystical thought, which, she said, when linked to the thought of Hellenism, of Stoicism, of Christianity, contributed to one identifying truth. It is her recognition of this overarching spiritual truth that inspires this entry in one of her notebooks: "There is no attitude of greater humility than to wait in silence and patience…. It is the patience which transmutes time into eternity. Total obedience to time obliges God to grant eternity."

In any case, it will be asserted that Babbitt would have found in Simone Weil some of the ambivalences that he perceived in George Sand. In particular, Simone Weil's obedience to the promptings of the soul would have been to him as excessive as George Sand's to the promptings of the heart. This reference to George Sand is at the same time helpful in establishing a positive connection between Babbitt and Simone Weil. For in George Sand, Babbitt did finally find cause for hope. He noted that towards the end of her career she was able to rescue the principle of belief from false ideals and to have a faith that outlived shocks of disillusion. In an age of great enlightenment and little light, Babbitt noted with satisfaction, George Sand managed to sustain "the contemplative sense wherein resides invincible faith." The same kind of interiorizing virtue he would have finally saluted in Simone Weil, who, dying at the age of thirty-four, never had the advantages of George

Sand's longevity.

Babbitt would have seen in Simone Weil a commitment to the discipline of ideas, as well as an intellectual honesty and a moral realism, that he believed to be indispensable to one who addresses oneself to the problems of the modern world. "The man who is spiritually strenuous," Babbitt writes in *Rousseau and Romanticism*, "has entered upon the 'path'.... Progress on the path may be known by its fruits—negatively by the extinction of the expansive desires ..., positively by an increase in peace, poise, centrality." Simone Weil's possession of the contemplative sense and her example of "spiritual strenuousness" would have earned her a revered place among Babbitt's "masters of modern French criticism." In her he would have discovered a defeat of Rousseauistic enthusiasm, an indictment of the variable and impressionistic element in literature and thought, a critical check against the centrifugal elements of originality and genius, and, above all, a defense of the belief that individualism starts not from rights but from obligations.

*The Need for Roots* is both a vindication and an updating of *Democracy and Leadership*. The false values that Simone Weil focuses on in history, in politics, in art, in religion, and in science are those that Babbitt warned against. The spirit of truth that Simone Weil finds absent from the whole of human thought is of a piece with that false intellectual pride that Babbitt saw displacing the order of moral character. For him, as later for Simone Weil, the historical actualities of this displacement impel reflection, or as he writes: "A consideration of man's ignorance and blindness as they are revealed on a vast scale in the facts of history gives a positive basis to humility." No two books could be more in agreement with respect to the cumulative effects unleashed upon man and society through the union of material efficiency and ethical and moral unrestraint. No two critics of modern society could be more in agreement with respect to the scientism that, subjecting man and verifying values according to the "law of thing," inspires divine discontent and romantic rootlessness, and delivers man into the hands of a blind collectivity.

Modern scientific materialism, which Babbitt connected with "the whole fatal circle of naturalism," has become identified with diminishing spiritual effort and increasing spiritual sloth. This form of science, which indicates for Simone Weil a dislodgement of religious contemplation, is for Babbitt an arrogant imperialism. It leads to what Babbitt calls "the efficient megalomaniac" and to that use of science which, in Burke's phrase, seeks to "improve the mystery of murder." It was to lead, Simone Weil concluded, directly to Hitler, in whom some of our own features are enlarged. Both concluded that what we build, in the long run, is an impregnable social machine. In effect, collective thought, collective measures, collective actions, collective mediocrity underline the dispossession of mind and body in the modern world. "The powerful means are oppressive," says Simone Weil, "the nonpowerful remain inoperative."

In their critical opinions Babbitt and Simone Weil disclose a moral centrality uncompromising in formulation and application. First principles and, equally, principles of order were, for both, transcendent principles of discovered truth: and ultimate criteria of judgment. Neither one could ever separate the creative imagination from the moral imagination. "I believe in the responsibility of the writers of recent years for the disaster of our time," Simone Weil declares—a declaration that conveys the intrinsic tone of moral severity in her critical responses. Indeed, she was consistently unsparing in her criticism of men of letters who "introduce into literature a Messianic afflatus wholly detrimental to its artistic purity." Like Babbitt she denounced the romantic attitude that has invaded and captured so much of the province of the modern literary imagination.

"Everybody is becoming tinged with eleutheromania," writes Babbitt in *The New Laokoon* (1910), "taken up with his rights rather than with his duties, more and more unwilling to accept limitations." His words here anticipate in a remarkable way the moral-critical standards that Simone Weil held to with astonishing tenacity. Babbitt in his time and Simone Weil in hers—and both were quintessentially of their time—subscribed to the moral view of the literary imagination as being successful according to the degree in which it affirms the "law of units, measure, purpose." For both, the excrescence of the romantic outlook and temper, impressionism and expressionism, for example, sabotaged the idea of value. Romanticism constituted, in short, a debauch, a crippling lapse of discipline, whether as a discipline of "humane concentration," in Babbitt's critical vein, or of an "absolute attention," in Simone Weil's.

In their critical determinations Babbitt and Simone Weil returned to the *exemplaria Graeca* for the paradigms of what the New Humanist calls "vital unity, vital measure, vital purpose." The ancient Greeks, he maintained, possessed humane standards, held flexibly, and effected mediation between the One and the Many. To be sure, Greek civilization, Babbitt admitted, disclosed the same problem of unrestraint that he believed was pervasive in modern society and that he described as the "barbaric violation of the law of measure." But he also revered in Hellenism the power to triumph over this problem through a combination of "exquisite measure" with "perfect spontaneity." Through such a combination man was at once "thoroughly disciplined and inspired."

Babbitt and Simone Weil were to condemn artists who promote the cult of personality, who usurp the function of spiritual guidance, generate easy morals, and tolerate base-

ness. In the end such artists violate the literary-critical catechesis that Simone Weil underlines in one of her finest
essays, "Beyond Personalism": "The man for whom the
development of personality is all that counts has totally
lost all sense of the sacred.... So far from its being his person, what is sacred in a human being is the impersonal in
him." Going even beyond Babbitt, she viewed the Gospels
as the last and finest expression of Greek genius, as the
*Iliad* is its first. In such a modern literature she, like
Babbitt, saw a diminution of "strength of soul" and capitu-
lation to self-deception. And, like Babbitt, she refused to
exempt literature from the categories of good and evil.
Both thus emphasized a transcending sapiential order of
art, whether as "the responsibility of writers" or as "morality and literature." Babbitt believed that "the problem of
beauty is inseparable from the ethical problem." Simone
Weil believed that art should give insight into moral
world-order and resist the seductive pathologies of the
modern age.

These two critics of twentieth-century culture and
society remind us of moral and critical standards. One of
the extraordinary qualities that they share, and one found
only in the greatest thinkers, is the ability to reflect the
whole of their work in each of its parts. Babbitt examined
"mind in the modern world" dialectically, from within a
university purview. Simone Weil, also a teacher—and, like
Babbitt, no doubt a great and fearless teacher,—chose to
examine the soul of the world, choosing to enter at every
available opportunity the cockpit of strife. Her choice was
hastened and heightened by the advancing crises of civilization that Babbitt detected in *Literature and the American
College*. Theirs was not so much a search for general principles of order as it was a demanding confirmation of
these. Moral toughness permeates their life and thought.
Stuart Sherman's complaint that "the path Babbitt asks us
to tread is only wide enough for one" is echoed in the com-

plaints against Simone Weil.

Her contention that "real genius is nothing else but the supernatural virtue of humility in the domain of thought," recalls for us a theory of literature that Babbitt relentlessly asserted in the totality of his writings. Her message that "the glossy surface of our civilization hides a real intellectual decadence" is Babbitt's. Her statement that "in every sphere, we seem to have lost the elements of intelligence: the ideas of limit, measure, proportion, relation, compassion, contingency, interdependence, interrelations of means and ends," epitomizes the impelling meaning of the critical mission of Irving Babbitt. Her insistence that "nothing concerns human life so essentially, for every man at every moment, as good and evil. When literature becomes deliberately indifferent to the opposition of good and evil, it betrays its function and forfeits all claim to excellence," is that insistence for which Babbitt has long been condemned by the philistines who continue to view him as a "suzerain of an elite-university literature department." Her charge that "culture…is an instrument manipulated by professors for manufacturing more professors, who in turn, will manufacture still more professors" is precisely Babbitt's indictment of that specialization that he equated with overemphasis and with a loss of a sense of proportion.

Babbitt has been called a "New England Saint" and Simone Weil a "Saint of the Churchless." In their perception of the world and in their conception of the meaning of life there is much to be found that endorses these honoring designations. Yet there is still another path of sympathy that they travelled. It marks a still higher ideational parallelism, and one that instances the highest point of the convergence of their thought. It relates to a definitive ethos, with its complex of civilized ideas and habits, its embodied moral beliefs and certitudes, its reverent apprehension of a spiritual unity and discipline of order, as well as an order of reality with a standard of value. Babbitt and Simone Weil labored to save this ethos from a modern world that, in its Promethean secularism, proclaims "the end of the modern world." Babbitt's moral centrality was born of earnestness, Simone Weil's, of grace—surely compatible and complementary centralities. Each spoke out bravely regarding the modern experience of affliction and shipwreck.

Men, Babbitt declares, "tend to come together in proportion to their intuitions of the One.... We ascend to meet." And Simone Weil insists: "Faith is above all the conviction that the good is one." As critics they refined their world view in the face of the active hostility of the times in which they lived—the hostility that, then and now, characterizes *la trahison des clercs*. Irving Babbitt and Simone Weil resisted and challenged the vaunting powers of betrayal and disbelief with a conviction and a vigor arising from the affirmation of a moral and spiritual ethos that achieves permanence among impermanent things. Their example, both as presentation and as interpretation, testifies to a double mission: the critical pursuit of truth and the search for salvation.

## CHAPTER FIVE

# Irving Babbitt
# and Richard Weaver

Two modern American teachers and critics who can now be honored as Sages and, indeed, included among the *Sacri Vates,* are Irving Babbitt and Richard Weaver (1910-1963). One who in any way studies two recently reissued books, Babbitt's *Character and Culture* (originally titled *Spanish Character and Other Essays*)[1] and Weaver's *Visions of Order,*[2] will need very little convincing as to the appropriateness of the sapiential ascription. To read these two books again, or even for the first time, is to make contact with men of vision who are quintessentially men of wisdom. Perhaps at no time of our history do we have more urgent need for wisdom than now. For the wisdom we gain here is both salvific and restorative; it enables us to climb the ladder of illumination. Babbitt likens this process to "the ascending path of insight and discrimination"; Weaver describes it as the need to "have something ascending up toward an ultimate source of good." This moving upward requires strenuous effort, and its rewards are to be found in the higher experiential contexts of what is self-cleansing and self-disciplining.

Moral indolence and apathy, both Babbitt and Weaver stress, are forces of gravity that need to be quelled if one is to fly beyond the nets of naturalism and temperamental excesses. Such ascent, Babbitt stresses, is an intrinsic part of the "aspiration to rise above the impermanent." He sees this entire process in the light of individual maturity and growth, and especially as to how this process relates to its development. Weaver is also emphatically aware of individual character, which he examines in direct relation to the larger cultural map, to what he designates as "the discriminations of a culture." It can be said that Babbitt addresses first and foremost the problem of man, of his character and destiny; Weaver, the problem of culture—"the cultural crisis of our time." To make this particular contrast is not to lessen Babbitt's larger civilizational concerns, even as his magisterial book *Democracy and Leadership* will thoroughly indicate. Still, in Babbitt the voice we hear is mainly that of the teacher speaking to his students. "For Babbitt's service as teacher," Austin Warren writes of his Harvard mentor, "transcended his doctrine." If Babbitt begins with *anthropos,* and Weaver begins with *paideia,* both ultimately meet in absolute allegiance to *humanitas,* which in the end allies them in their search for *aristeia* of character and culture.

Of Weaver, Russell Kirk remarks, with characteristic pungency and insight: "Meant to expose and restrain the illusions of our century, his books and his teaching were instruments for action." He goes on to say that, for Weaver, order was an "austere passion: the inner order of the soul, the outer order of society." These words could equally apply to that great conservative mind in the earlier years of the twentieth century, Babbitt. Neither Babbitt nor Weaver ceased to seek after principles of order in a century of disorder. For Babbitt the Great War of 1914-1918 emblematized the symptoms and portents of modern disorder, even as he, an admirer of Aristotle, goes back to Jean Jacques Rousseau as the primary architect of the scheme of disorder in the modern world in the form of unchecked romanticism. For Weaver, World War II unmasked the spirit of disorder, and he, an admirer of Plato, goes back to William of Ockham (1285-1349) as a progenitor of disorder in the form of nominalism. To view Babbitt and Weaver together, in continuity, so to speak, is to view two visionary thinkers deeply concerned with the order of a humane civilization and the order of human character. In their conjoining perceptions and interpretations of the rhythm of disintegration and the schism of the soul they centered on the crisis of modernism as a crisis of disorder.

What especially ties together these two thinkers is their defense of the idea of order as it affects the personal realm and the socio-cultural realm. And what both sought to find as a coalescing force in the two realms was the element of stability, or that integral metaphysical force which checks the impulse of disorder that never ceases to assault life. Their writings, whatever the differences in style and in specificities of emphasis, are responsive to the virtue of character—the character of man, the character of culture, the character of the polity. For them character signifies discipline of responsibility, the moral sense and burden of responsibility, to be more exact. And for them such discipline predicates a categorical need for standards in direct relation to what Babbitt calls an "enduring scale of values" and a "clear-cut scale of moral values."

No modern American critics have been more aware of an interdependent need for discipline and standards than Babbitt and Weaver. Babbitt views this double need in terms of man's discovery of the path that leads to human growth, maturity, edification. Traveling on this path mandates effort and choice of direction, or as Babbitt cogently describes it in one of his essays, "Interpreting India to the West":

> On the one hand is the ascending path of insight and discrimination. Those who take it may be termed the spiritual athletes. On the other hand is the descending

path towards the subrational followed by those who court the confused reverie that comes from the breakdown of barriers and the blurring of distinctions and who are ready to forego purpose in favor of "spontaneity"; and these may be termed the cosmic loafers.

Weaver, in his own vision of order, is writing along these same lines of thought, with respect to the principle of distinction, when he declares: "In order to have meaningful status we must have something ascending toward an ultimate source of good." In ancient times, it was Plato who viewed the need and possibility of standards in the light of what he called the problem of the One and the Many. Once again, Babbitt is to the point here: "Unless there is something that abides in the midst of change and serves to measure it, it is obvious that there can be no standards." Babbitt and Weaver were to indict the arch tendency in modern times as the tendency to drift in centerless, undisciplined, anarchic ways. In this tendency Babbitt saw the manifestation of disorder in the form of anarchy, and Weaver, in the form of presentism. And for both disorder was rooted in what Weaver perceived, in words that echo those of Babbitt, as "the confusion of categories" and indifference, or hostility, to "transcendental ideas":

> ...the greatest weakness of a function-oriented culture is that it sets little or no store by the kind of achievement which is comparatively timeless—the formation of character, the perfection of style, the attainment of distinction in intellect and imagination. These require for their appreciation something other than keen senses; they require an effort of the mind and the spirit to grasp timeless values, to perceive the presence of things that extend through a temporal span.

Clearly, Babbitt and Weaver were reacting, with intense

and total concern, to the main issues of contemporary life as expressed in literature, politics, education, and religion. And on these issues they spoke out candidly, consistently. In many ways they were diagnosticians of modern social order in rapid and mindless retreat from a faith in first principles and first causes—in "the law of the spirit," "the law of measure" steadily being supplanted by a "new dualism based on the myth of man's natural goodness." Babbitt and Weaver associated this retreat with the forces of aggressive anarchy and revolution assaulting the foundations of Western civilization, and especially its humanistic tradition. These forces, secular and gnostic, as well as decadent and ideological in orientation and intent, conspire to bring about, in Weaver's words, "the progressive demotion of man." These are precisely the forces that now embody the nihilism that pervades the basic categories of life and discards all semblance of the truth of the inner life. Babbitt and Weaver rendered in their own particular eras the ongoing stages of modern disequilibrium and deorientation which have now reached a point of no return. In their rendering of what Babbitt sees as a modern world "treading very near the edge of sudden disaster," one hears the prophetic voice crying out with the urgency and the fearlessness that belong to the ethical prophet's mission.

We hear this voice in the final paragraph of the final essay, "The Reconsideration of Man," in *Visions of Order,* Weaver speaking here with genuine vatic intensity about culture as an intermediary between man and his highest vocation, which he also reminds us is a matter of spirit:

> There is always in a cultural observance a little gesture of piety, a recognition that there are higher demands on man along with the lower. While culture is not a worship and should not be made a worship, it is a kind of orienting of the mind toward mood, a reverence for the spirit on secular occasions.

And in Babbitt, too, the prophetic voice can be heard with equal intensity of attention to what Rabbi Abraham J. Heschel has called "the application of timeless standards to particular situations" and "an interpretation of a particular moment in history." Babbitt writes:

> As for the typical modern, he is not only at an infinite remove from anything resembling renunciation, but is increasingly unable to accept the will to refrain from anything else on a basis of mere tradition and authority. Yet the failure to exercise the will to refrain in some form or degree means spiritual anarchy. A combination such as we are getting more and more at present of spiritual anarchy with an ever-increasing material efficiency—power without wisdom, as one is tempted to put it—is not likely to work either for the happiness of the individual or for the welfare of society.

As teachers in the highest moral and civilizational sense, Babbitt and Weaver believed in the education of the whole human personality—intellect, character, mind, and soul. (Babbitt's first book, *Literature and the American College,* argued forcefully for what Claes Ryn, in his discerning introduction to *Character and Culture,* calls a "reinvigorated humanistic curriculum and discipline as a way of reversing the decline of Western life and letters.") To the very end of his life and career, Babbitt's preoccupation with educational issues never wavered. And, no less than Babbitt, Weaver argued vigorously the case for humane letters. In a celebrated essay, "Up from Liberalism" (1958-1959), he wrote in words echoing Babbitt's own, "[O]ur education will have to recover the lost vision of the person as a creature of both intellect and will." "Gnostics of Education," the longest essay in *Visions of Order,* and inspired by Eric Voegelin's *The New Science of Politics* (1952), conveys the essence of Weaver's educational thought and views.

Both in Babbitt's and in Weaver's writings, educational problems have an intrinsic bearing on their major ideas and thought. Their opinions are directed not only to their students in the classroom but also to their auditors at large. Their own teaching experiences doubtlessly helped to inspire and even define their educational thought, even as they treated educational issues as a significant part of the modern cultural scene. What they witness in the realm of education inevitably affects, even molds, their view of society and culture, and, of course, the human condition in the modern age. And what they have to say about education, whether diagnostic, censorial, or corrective, is clear and direct, singularly constructive and not cynical. In their educational ideas one finds the saving qualities of measure, prudence, humility. It is the teacher as sage who discourses here, guided in lecture and text by a sense of proportionateness and by a need, in Babbitt's words, "to glimpse the total symmetry of life and with reference to this symmetry to maintain some degree of poise and centrality." And here, too, one has the privilege of listening to a true humanist, in contradistinction to our modern specialists, the Napoleons of solution, with their overemphasis and glitz.

Babbitt and Weaver illustrate a common concern and a common witness to the crisis of education in the twentieth century and the accelerating diminution of human values and humane learning. Babbitt largely examines the causes of educational malaise; Weaver is responding to effects. Their writings on education constitute a united front against what Russell Kirk speaks of as the decadence of higher learning in America. In their discernments we have an astonishing portrayal of the theories and movements that have contributed to our educational plight, today epitomized by anarchic and nihilistic conditions at all levels of American education. Babbitt's essay on "President Eliot and American Education" (1929) remains indispensable testimony for anyone who seeks to understand some of the basic reasons why American education has been floundering for many decades now. One will want to reflect on what Babbitt has to say, with such a timely ring of truth and perception, in these representative observations:

> The humanitarian idealism based on the faith in progress will be found on analysis to be either utilitarian or sentimental. Practically, in education as elsewhere, a utilitarian and sentimental movement has been displacing traditions that are either religious or humanistic.

> In the absence of humane purposes, what has triumphed is the purpose of the utilitarian. A multitude of specialties...has taken the place not only of the selection of studies in the old curriculum but of the selective principle itself. Education has become increasingly miscellaneous and encyclopaedic.

> At the bottom of the whole educational debate...is the opposition between a religious-humanistic and a utilitarian-sentimental philosophy. This opposition, involving as it does first principles, is not subject to compromise or mediation. Those who attempt such mediation are not humanists but Laodiceans.

Babbitt's indictment of a raw and uncivilized pragmatism afflicting education returns us to his endorsement of Matthew Arnold's contention that our democracy is too much concerned with quantity and not quality. American democracy has obviously chosen to enforce, in an imperial manner, quantified reductionisms in the shape of what Babbitt calls "naturalistic disintegration," as part of the effort to legislate equality and uniformity. And a sham liberalism, as Babbitt reminds us in *Democracy and Leadership*, by not distinguishing between moral and material progress, has misled modern man to place ironclad faith in organization, efficiency, machinery: in short, in utilitarian and utopian schemes that have now emerged in the adulterated metaphysics of a New Morality and a New Age. Inevitably, these schemes produce the momentum of subversions that affects the educational realm. Weaver addresses these subversions in his essay "Gnostics of Education," updating Babbitt's earlier critical testimony by giving to it a more current garb and idiom. That is to say, he helps take Babbitt's testimony beyond pragmatism by bringing it into contact with an educational system now being gradually annexed by those he dubs "radical doctrinaires and social faddists." Weaver, in other words, provides us with a picture of educational dissimulation, *in extremis,* as it advances from pragmatism to ideology.

For Weaver, as for Babbitt, the central function of education is twofold: to form character and to preserve culture. But this function, he asserts, has been seriously impaired by the growth of progressivist educational philosophy in the hands of "revolutionaries" and "in the form of a systematic attempt to undermine a society's traditions and beliefs through the educational establishment." These revolutionaries, he goes on to say, have a vision of a "new future" totally unlike and even hostile to the past. They seek, above all, to nullify a vision of order that Weaver associates with the classical and Judaeo-Christian patrimony of the West. Among the aims of these revolutionaries he counts the methodical erasure of a common body of knowledge, of accepted truths, of standards, of authority as the most crippling. The following observation, written more than thirty years ago, and strikingly reechoing Babbitt, underlines Weaver's perception of the kind of ideology that today dominates educational thought and practice: "The student is to be prepared not to save his soul, or to inherit the wisdom and usages of past civilizations, or even to get ahead in life, but to become a member of a utopia resting on a false view of both nature and man." Weaver connects this modern subversive educational movement by way of historical descent with the Gnosticism of the first and second centuries A.D., the main goal, then and now, being to restructure humane values and concepts in terms suited to an "enlightenment" that boasts of being above creation, and that also avows that the material universe in and of itself is the real source of evil. The educationists of the new order, Weaver contends, parallel the Gnostics of antiquity in promulgating "a kind of irresponsibility to the past and to the structure of reality in the present."

The Rousseauism of Babbitt thus assumes in Weaver the shape of Gnosticism; the consequences for both are epitomized in disorder. Certainly what Weaver has to say in the following statement regarding the deification of man and the radicalization of the whole system of ethics into something that becomes categorically man-centered has definitive parallel, in language and in thought, in Babbitt's *Rousseau and Romanticism:*

> The Gnostic belief was that man is not sinful, but divine. The real evil in the universe cannot be imputed to him; his impulses are good, and there is no ground for restraining him from anything he wants to do…. By divinizing man, Gnostic thinking says that what he wants to do, he should do.

Present-day Gnostics of education, Weaver further observes, and again further confirming Babbitt's views, reject the existence or relevance of any moral absolutes as these affect and determine rightness from wrongness. Modern educationists, hence, show little or no regard for an existent reality, but rather for "the mastery of methodology"—for the technique and the technicism that currently hold sway in educational agenda. What Weaver is obviously criticizing is exactly the modern temper, and process, that Babbitt saw as the shifting of a value-system increasingly controlled by the metaphysicians of the Many who have defeated the metaphysicians of the One; who have defeated, in short, the acceptance of what must be a central premise in grappling strenuously with the problem of the One and the Many.

In his examination of modern education, in particular, and of culture in general, it can be said, Weaver traces the consequences of what happens to the human world when there is no principle of unity and, in turn, no standards. He singles out in the process of what he depicts as "the dark night of the mind" the effects of unlimited democracy, about which Babbitt has trenchant things to say in his essay on "The Problem of Style in a Democracy," composed originally as an address to The American Academy of Arts and Letters, November 10, 1932, included in *Character and Culture*. Weaver argues that "When democracy is taken from its proper place and is allowed to fill the entire horizon, it produces an envious hatred not only of all distinction but of all difference." This contention, though in a more contemporary vein, continues Babbitt's argument that "Another and far graver error is to seek, like the equalitarian democrat, to get rid of the selective and aristocratic principle altogether. The cult of the common man that the equalitarian democrat encourages, is hard to distinguish from commonness." Any reflecting on the following sentences in the chapter "Democracy and Standards," in *Democracy and Leadership*, should remind one that Irving Babbitt and Richard Weaver finally speak in one voice:

> The democratic contention that everybody should have a chance is excellent provided it mean that everybody is to have a chance to measure up to high standards. If the democratic extension of opportunity is, on the other hand, made a pretext for lowering standards, democracy is, insofar, incompatible with civilization.

Babbitt and Weaver focus on John Dewey's extensive role in the "denigration of the intellect," and see in his exaltation of activity over thinking a ruinous departure from the great body of traditional knowledge and the wisdom of the race. Babbitt sees Dewey's influence in a national tendency among educators to insist on "the doctrine of service" at the expense of culture and civilization, and of character and the inner life. Weaver sees Dewey's impact on educational theory and policy as one that above all discards the significant place of the concepts, signs, and symbols through which man has created cultural achievements. The results bring about an extreme and expansive secularization and with it the arrogant dismissal of moral, spiritual, and religious principles, especially as these inhere in the virtue of piety and the role it plays in "the discipline of the negative," as Weaver expresses it and then goes on to add, again evoking Babbitt's thinking and idiom: "Effective education often demands the rigorous suppressing of a present, desultory interest so that we can focus on things that have a real, enduring, and sanctioned interest. Indeed, this is identical with the act of concentration." In remarkably prophetic ways, then, Babbitt and Weaver perceived not only the growing eclipse of excellence throughout American education, but also the breakdown of authority. This process of decomposition, which Weaver connects with "the substitution of fantasy for historicity," and which Babbitt was to connect with reverie, "this imaginative melting of man into outer nature," is quintessentialized in Weaver's picture of the teacher in America under incessant and heavy attack:

> ...the teacher is not to be viewed as one in authority commissioned to instruct, but as a kind of moderator whose function is merely to conduct a meeting. Especially resented is the idea that the teacher has any advantage of knowledge or wisdom which entitles him

to stand above his students. This would be a recognition of inequality, and equality must reign, *ruat caelum!*

Inevitably Babbitt and Weaver are indicting the rise of political ideology as it afflicts not only American character and culture, but also the organic conception of man and his world. Political ideology becomes, in effect, the haven of "the enemies of the permanent things." Man, Babbitt and Weaver insist, may be classified as a political animal, but political activity is not his nor his culture's highest expression, or as Weaver declares: "He [man] is also a contemplative animal, and a creature with aesthetic and cultural yearnings. His very restlessness is a sign that he is a spiritual being with intimations about his origin and destiny." *Character and Culture* and *Visions of Order* have, in effect, the power of reminding us that Babbitt and Weaver wrestled unceasingly with the primary questions. They particularly lamented Americans' growing submission to what Babbitt terms a "cheap contemporaneousness," and what Weaver designates as "the belief that only existence in the present can give significance to a thing." This belief inevitably denies the place of memory as that which, Weaver submits, "directs one along the path of obligation" and keeps "us whole and consistent in opposition to that contrary force which is dissolution."

"It is the critic's business," Babbitt writes, "to grapple with the age in which he lives and give it what he sees it needs." These words best define the critical calling not only of Babbitt but also of Weaver, and underline the courage a true critic needs to establish a moral ethos in examining life, literature, and thought. Babbitt and Weaver never deviated from their critical calling, even as their writings show a centrality and a consistency that invest their standards and outlook with an integrity of purpose and vision. To the dignity of literature they join the dignity of criticism. What will most impress readers of these two books is the moral seriousness and responsibility, as well as the moral measure, which Babbitt and Weaver record in their writings, and which in turn make them profoundly credible as critics who have something important to say about the human condition, and inevitably to say something of value about the "war in the cave," that unending struggle in man between good and evil. No less than the moral imagination, moral criticism has the capacity to make men and women better in their cities in that special context Babbitt apprehends when he stresses that the indefinite future progress of humanity is unequal in importance to the immediate definite progress of the individual.

The problems that Babbitt associates with "the present contagion of commonness" and its impact on cultural life are problems that Weaver addressed remedially. For Babbitt the loss of a sense of proportion, especially as seen in the unchecked growth of specialization, constituted a severe crisis of culture inherent in the crisis of modernity. And for Weaver the loss of historical consciousness is tantamount to his fear that persuasive speech, as an "ethics of rhetoric," is to be displaced by mere communication. Both critics speak as one in rejecting what Weaver calls "the principle of pure relativism for cultures." And both are profoundly aware of a modern world that, through its machine culture, has fallen into idolatry. "But the road away from idolatry," Weaver observes, "remains the same as before: it lies in respect for the struggling dignity of man and for his orientation toward something higher than himself which he has not created."

What best reconciles letters and life? This question much preoccupied both critics, and both emphasized the role of the ethical faculty in judging cultural forms. Truly ethical art is at once imaginative and decorous, Babbitt insisted, noting in *Rousseau and Romanticism* that

> The presence of the ethical imagination whether in art or life is always known as an element of calm.... But it

is only with reference to some ethical centre that we may determine what art is soundly recreative, in what forms of adventure the imagination may innocently indulge.

Weaver is no less insistent on the need for ethical apprehensions of social-cultural creations and forms that are imposed but that are not worth the cost and have no real validity:

So it is that when a culture falls to the worshipping of the forms it has created, it grows blind to the source of cultural expression itself and may engender perverse cruelty. The degeneration may take the form of static arts, of barbarous legal codes in defense of conventions, or the inhuman sacrifice exacted by a brilliant technology. At some point, its delight in these things has clouded over the right ethical and other determinations of life.

Modern Western culture and society, Babbitt and Weaver agreed, can be increasingly identified by its tyranny of forms, equipped with a new language and new clothes, and driven by an oppressive bureaucracy and a new technology. For both critics, Americans' easy acceptance of and subservience to these reifying forms instanced the sharp intellectual and spiritual decline of a nation and its people. "[A]ny granting of moral status and imperative force to form in its spatiotemporal embodiment is a sign of danger," Weaver warned. The only way a culture, he went on to say, can be kept from " 'worshipping monuments of its own magnificence,' " thus becoming repressive and destructive even in the midst of great achievements, is to recognize and preserve what he calls "allocations of the spirit": "For if man is a cognitive, aesthetic, ethical, and religious creature, he must maintain some rights of office among these various

faculties." No less than Babbitt, Weaver observed a pronounced tendency to extremism in American life, and he
repeatedly warned against this tendency as he saw it
asserted in all aspects of American society and culture. At
the heart of this extremism he viewed a growing pattern of
disorder in reckless deviations from the sacred path that
Babbitt saw as leading to peace, poise, and centrality.
Weaver especially lamented the modern world's "general
exaltation of means over ends," as people more and more
"feel a loyalty toward means which leaves them indifferent
to ends.""The more secular society grows," he warned, "the
more dominant this attitude is likely to become."

Babbitt's enemies have liked to think that he left no followers or allies and that he exerted little or no influence
after his death in 1933. Such are, everywhere and always,
the fantasies of the liberal mind. No two books, separated
in date of publication by over thirty years, more forcefully
repudiate these fantasies than *Character and Culture* and
*Visions of Order*. In their basic themes and ethos, these
books demonstrate astonishing continuity and correlation.
In their warnings regarding the health of American character and culture, they depict a shared indictment of
tendencies that have progressively led a nation and its people to chase after the heresies and the illusions that have no
purpose other than that of destroying both the idea of
value and humane civilization.

Babbitt discerned and identified the modern malaise as
it was developing and spreading with cruel rapidity. His
teachings and writings sought to chart those regions of
modernity that held the greatest danger for modern man.
Critical fortitude, steadfastness, and patience characterize
his life and work. He pressed on with his mission, his calling, to the end, refusing to be stranded, like others, on "the
heights of despair." For Babbitt the law of humility was
endless. With Edmund Burke he believed that it is at the
root of all other virtues that involve first principles.

"Nothing will avail short of humility," Babbitt insisted. Babbitt stands at the fountain-head of the dissident critical spirit that modernity and all its sectaries could not mute. "In the closing years of the twentieth century," Ryn observes, "it is evident that Irving Babbitt will go down in history as one of his country's original and seminal intellects." One could go so far as to say that the crisis of modernity, as it now slides with a vengeance into a postmodern stage of decadence and nihilism, cannot be fully grasped or resisted without an understanding of Babbitt's achievement.

Even to ponder a few pages from Babbitt's oeuvre each day can be a valuable exercise for anyone who wants to be rescued from contemporary negators of the moral life and the ethical life: from, in a word, the technological-Benthamite forces of gravity. Ultimately Babbitt's thought has a good influence, imparting as it does soundness and sanity, good sense, reasonableness, direction, balance— reverent qualities that actively oppose the disordering extremes that modern life legislates indiscriminately. He was truly a critical genius who was for too long misunderstood and misrepresented, unrecognized and unrewarded by his countrymen. But abroad, especially in the Orient, he was esteemed as an American sage and saint who had wrought a noble reconciliation of East and West, of Confucius and Aristotle, of Buddha and Christ.

Nowhere in his published writings does Weaver acknowledge straightaway Babbitt's influence or praise its significance—perhaps because great thinkers prefer their own counsel and seek to protect and preserve their own sovereignty of mind and thought. On one occasion when Weaver does mention Babbitt's name (along with Paul Elmer More's), in an essay entitled "Agrarianism in Exile" (1950), it is on a disparaging note that, following T.S. Eliot and Allen Tate, simply re-states "the fallacy of humanism." In "its admission of a theism," Weaver writes,

Agrarianism is "unafraid to step beyond the phenomenal world," whereas the New Humanism "assumed that man could find his destiny through a discriminating study of his own achievements." At the time of Weaver's composition of "Agrarianism in Exile," it hardly needs saying, Babbitt's achievement had not as yet been honestly estimated so as to disprove many of his critics' attacks on his ideas as lacking the idea of transcendence, of the absolute, of a total awareness. Yet, as *Visions of Order* shows so conclusively, Weaver had pondered his Babbitt, reacted to his ideas, and even used his language. Indeed, as a young graduate student he had studied his Babbitt in order to complete a master's thesis in English, in the spring of 1934, at Vanderbilt University, under the direction of John Crowe Ransom. That thesis was entitled "The Revolt Against Humanism," and in it he voiced doubts about "the creed of the genteel tradition" later articulated in "Agrarianism in Exile."

But when one chooses to go beyond the early and disingenuous criticisms of Babbitt and the New Humanism, which had no doubt brushed Weaver's generation, one will discover that Babbitt's moral impact was deep and lasting, even as any critical comparison of *Character and Culture* and *Visions of Order* will prove. Yes, differences in critical orientation are there, but the affinities and the similarities, the visionary *sperma,* the larger moral concerns and spiritual purposes are also very much there, transcendently. The passage of time—Babbitt had been dead for more than three decades when *Visions of Order* saw print—had softened some of the immediate intellectual tensions and hostilities, personal animosities and regional differences, that had clouded Babbitt's contribution. His central message to modern man, his wise teachings, and the universality of his vision could hardly escape either the interest or the respect of a great inheritor and continuer: Richard Weaver was, after all, fighting the new-old battles, now even more perilous in their outcome, in which Babbitt had fought valiantly and selflessly, in the front lines, in the fledgling years of the twentieth century.

In his unrelenting labors to provide correctives to the fragmentation and excesses of the modern world, Babbitt had penetrated to its heart of darkness. *Visions of Order,* in its remarkable way, pays tribute to Babbitt's enduring legacy and relevance. Babbitt neither desired nor expected to be acknowledged for his contribution to life and letters. There is, really, no need to cite him by name: his ideas have both implicit and beneficent consequences, and cannot be routinely relegated to footnotes. Weaver is among those "keen-sighted few" who attest to Irving Babbitt's permanence of value in the order of the "permanent things."

## CHAPTER SIX

# The Widening of the Circle

**“T**hough frequently misunderstood and maligned, Babbitt is likely to live on after most of his critics have faded from memory.”These words appear in Professor Claes G. Ryn's *Will, Imagination and Reason: Irving Babbitt and the Problem of Reality* (1986). Ryn's main critical concern is with Babbitt's ideas in relation to moral and aesthetic responsibility, and he seeks to mold these ideas “into a systematic whole, thus developing a new approach to the problem of knowledge.” Babbitt possessed unwavering standards as these affect and mold concepts of will, imagination, and reason and ultimately define “a comprehensive view of life.”The fact remains that Babbitt's moral and aesthetic standards are not perceived as being viable in the modern world, are too severe and demanding for a society dominated by egalitarian, formalistic, and ahistorical forces. Clearly, Babbitt's views in their power and conviction require a total commitment of discipline and belief that goes counter to the vagaries of the modern temper. It is the singular strength of Ryn's important book that it both recognizes Babbitt as a classic and enhances his meaning in our time.

Babbitt grappled mightily with basic philosophical problems, but it must also never be forgotten that he is, first and foremost, a man of ideas—a man of letters, to be more exact. And a man of letters insofar as he speaks to the total human condition is a generalist, a universalist, whose mission and message are not confined to any one intellectual theory or epistemological synthesis. As Allen Tate writes in "The Man of Letters in the Modern World":

> The general intelligence is the intelligence of the man of letters: he must not be committed to the illiberal specializations that the nineteenth century has proliferated into the modern world: specializations in which means are divorced from ends, action from sensibility, matter from mind, society from the individual, religion from moral agency, love from lust, poetry from thought, communion from experience, and mankind in the community from men in the crowd.[1]

Any attempt to systematize Babbitt's thought must in fact be viewed as a methodological endeavor to locate and define that thought in selective parameters. Babbitt was, to be sure, a moralist who, as he wrote of Matthew Arnold, is ever aware that "in addition to his ordinary self of passing impulse and desire...has a permanent self that is felt in relation to his ordinary self as a power of control." He was not a builder of systems, and he was not a systematist. We may choose to see his achievement in its systematic orientation and phases, but that view does not tell the whole story or capture the organic meaning of Babbitt's writings. Even a cursory review of his writings underlines the need to see Babbitt as a positive and critical humanist who, like Arnold, achieves the union of imagination and reason. In the end Babbitt must be seen as an exemplary teacher-critic whose text comes from the "alphabet of the universal spirit" and whose piety is for the "fathers," for what Goethe calls "tradition" and "those revered values by which the remote is bound, the torn made whole."[2] Like Goethe, Babbitt is a thinker and a sage, but not a philosopher or an ideologue.

In his attacks on proliferating specialization in the intellectual disciplines, Babbitt was unwavering. It much behooves us, now that more scholars are "revisiting" Babbitt's writings, to protect him from those who would transform him into a specialized academic commodity. The scholar's responsibility today is to interpret the whole of Babbitt in ways that would make his ideas more assimilative in the American mind and that would reinterpret his writings so that their wisdom and insight would be more readily absorbed in critical discourse. The civilizing value of Babbitt's ideas needs to be communicated by his interpreters in relation to culture and society and to become, as it were, an intrinsic and dynamic part of our critical heritage.

*Will, Imagination and Reason,* in concept and content, is not an easy book to read and its appeal will be confined to a limited audience. It is a book to be pondered, a quintessentially serious and profound book that stands in a great European intellectual tradition strongly opposed to a mathematically oriented naturalism and positivism and that bears the marks of the Swedish philosopher Folke Leander (1910-1981), Ryn's Swedish mentor—the "Optimus Doctor" to whom the book is dedicated.[3] The dedicatory inscription is altogether appropriate, especially because *Will, Imagination and Reason* is based on Leander's own skeletal outlines, suggestions, and analysis of Babbitt's central ideas. Illness did not permit Leander to go beyond preliminary explorations of Babbitt's thought. By 1981 Ryn had written the first manuscript draft of this book, reworking, developing, and integrating Leander's original materials into a larger whole.

During the years since Leander's death, as Ryn tells us in a prefatory reminiscence, the manuscript was revised and rewritten and now stands on its own, the early drafts indistinguishable from his own thought and writing, though allegiant to the original, collaborative goal of exploring "the relationship between Babbitt's ethical and aesthetic ideas and the implications of that relationship for how we understand reality and the knowledge of reality." That goal is admirably achieved in *Will, Imagination and Reason*. No scholar in the future will now be hampered by an inadequate assessment of Babbitt's philosophical explorations. If the immediate circle of readers of Ryn's book will be small, it will also be a grateful and influential circle that will in turn serve to create a widening circle of readers and, hopefully, catechists.

What Ryn indicates, above all, is that Babbitt possessed philosophical and spiritual qualities that ennobled his ideas and distinguished them from those who, like John Dewey and his followers, failed to observe the ethical element in man's moral and theoretical nature that transcends change. This book helps to show us that a genuine man of ideas exposes those forms of moral sloppiness that constitute a decadent romanticism and lead us deeper into what Babbitt termed "zones of illusion." It should also help us to extend and deepen our understanding of how Babbitt fuses intellectual breadth and philosophical depth, as well as ethical and moral functions. This synthesis is especially needful in a modern world in which moral standards and traditions are victims of the *élan vital* that Babbitt associates with man's expansive desires, which impede due restraint and proportion within individual and national life.

Babbitt's authenticity as a man of letters, as well as his pedagogical and critical ardor, need to be doubly stressed when false men of letters are cheaply manufactured in the intellectual community. In Babbitt, in the larger man and the deeper nature, we have the real thing; he establishes standards that separate what is genuine from what is spurious. It is this Babbitt who needs most to reside in American life and letters if his values and virtues are to have visible impact on the crisis of modernity that grinds on at a furious and even fateful pace. To view the contemporary shapers of the liberalistic order—to view, that is, their mediocrity and superciliousness, but also their false and yet acclaimed power and influence in all facets of culture and society—makes Babbitt's thought invaluable as a corrective force in the inner and outer life of the commonwealth.

Everything in our national life and thought today defies the moral prescriptions of Babbitt's teachings and writings; defies what Ryn crystallizes in these words: "Great art has a higher function, that is, a higher purpose, in the economy of the spirit." The application of the "inner check" that Babbitt and Paul Elmer More counseled as an ought is rejected by a society that eleutheromania has turned on its head. It will be difficult to turn things around, the difficulty itself being compounded by the worship of the new gods of megatechnics. The current deconstructionist craze that possesses higher education is symptomatic of the obstacles facing those few who champion Babbitt's goals for attaining "centrality of vision." The conditions of American life that Babbitt prophetically diagnosed in *Democracy and Leadership* (1924) have steadily declined, so much so that the law of numbers that Babbitt feared has now metamorphosed into the law of decadence, which D. H. Lawrence once described as a "greasy slipping into decay." If the America of the twenties and thirties was antagonistic to Babbitt, the America of the eighties and nineties is inevitably even more antagonistic! This sad fact must be kept in mind when reading Ryn's book. And it must be kept in mind particularly in the creation of any strategies for the recrudescence of Babbitt's worth to contemporary civilization.

Ryn's book emboldens us to persevere in our ambitions, and in our strategies, to reintegrate Babbitt's importance. At the same time we cannot be overly optimistic as to the outcome of our labors as we witness the ever-dizzying flux of modern life—the crass habits of mind and character, the lapses in conscience and conduct that ossify and signal the anarchies and the nihilisms assaulting all levels of human existence. Ryn's efforts (and those of his friends and allies) must be viewed in that context that T. S. Eliot recognizes when he declares that "we fight rather to keep something alive than in the expectation that anything will triumph."[4] Babbitt himself would not want us to be misled by any illusions concerning the possibility of a grand triumph; and he would not want us to misjudge irreducible realities of existence that he connects with the "immediate data of consciousness."

Ryn asserts that Babbitt's books "present thought about experience." His commentary enables one to pinpoint and evaluate more definitely Babbitt's humanistic concepts and distinctions. Though Babbitt did not systematically think through the subject of conceptual knowledge, as Ryn discloses, he nonetheless perceived the unsettling phenomenon in modern life of the man of science who becomes a "mere rationalist" and distorts experience for practical ends and thus ignores the place of the part in the experiential whole. Ryn is sometimes wary of Babbitt's inattention to the epistemological basis of his own ideas, but this wariness tends to obscure the fact that Babbitt was a man of letters and not a trained philosopher. It is a criticism that ascribes to Babbitt a particular function that he himself never pretended to possess. "I am merely a critic," he replied to those of his followers who sought to make of him something more than he was. We cannot, and should not, expect a man of letters to be more than what he is, though it should also be said, in all fairness to Ryn's thesis, that Babbitt in his response to pragmatism was closer to an epistemology than he realized. Ryn's interpretations remind us why Babbitt's importance to us has never been fully ascertained, and that is because he had particular theories about ethical wisdom and universal values. Ryn makes an observation that cannot be dismissed: "But until such theories become aware of and can defend their own epistemological foundation, they must lack confidence in philosophical debates and ultimately fail in the task of persuasion." Clearly this task belongs not to the man of letters but to his commentators, and it is a task in which Ryn excels.

Perhaps the greatest interior value of *Will, Imagination and Reason* is that it leads one to grasp the permanent significance of Babbitt's perception of the facts of moral life and order. This perception, however, was that of a man of letters who did not presume to develop what Babbitt himself termed "a complete and closed system." Ryn remarks that "if he [Babbitt] had gone on to philosophize about the epistemological status of his own thought, the result would have been an explicitly systemic approach and a logic of philosophy." Babbitt's "scant interest in questions of philosophical logic" is, for Ryn, cause for regret and calls for the kind of complements, refinements, or revisions that Ryn provides with precision and authority. It is not so much a modified as a strengthened Babbitt who emerges from Ryn's study. The augmentation, as it is developed in this book, is that of a friendly critic seeking to assess Babbitt's thought and its relevance to the crisis of modern civilization.

*Will, Imagination and Reason* impressively demonstrates that Babbitt had the capacity to be an "enlightener" and "enlarger." Regrettably, the special critical purpose and approach of Ryn's book do not also more fully reveal a Babbitt who transcended his doctrine precisely because he was a man of letters. Hence, to say as does Ryn that Babbitt's collected writings can be described as a "twentieth-century phenomenology of the mind" needlessly complicates the contribution of a man of letters. To be sure, Ryn is persuasive in showing that "Ideas are given new emphases, until a virtual transformation has been effected"; that "In every act of interpretation thought continues"; that "Weaknesses and strengths are discovered in the old formulations." But the philosophical and theoretical *foci* and truths of his book, as forceful as they are, tend to subordinate Babbitt's generalism. Doubtlessly the philosophical concepts that Ryn rearticulates and reformulates help to weed out mistakes and confusions. And doubtlessly his belief that "Human knowledge is a perpetual straining towards greater clarity and precision" attains an eloquent substance. Ryn's interpretations are invariably illuminating, but their hermeneutical nature deprives Babbitt of the humanistic constituents that shaped and stamped his teaching and writing in their sinuous reciprocity and unity. In a curious way, as we are reminded here, Babbitt's significance becomes perhaps too much a province of the very academy that has always found his ideas threatening. In one way, then, Ryn adds to this paradox, though he does so in a positive way insofar as the moral concerns of his book establish a conclusive and overarching critical commitment of the first order.

Babbitt, as Ryn emphasizes, regarded ethical action as the final answer to questions of reality. And this action constituted a moral effort—individual moral effort and the exercise of the "higher will," or "power of control." Moral goodness was for Babbitt the end of life since it is in goodness that one finds happiness and peace. Ryn's discussion of Babbitt's conception of the inner check rescues this aspect of Babbitt's thinking from confusion and misunderstanding, as well as from the behaviorists and naturalistic psychologists, "the chief enemies of human nature." In short, for Babbitt ethical will has primacy over intellect, or as Ryn states: "Moral standards are in a sense the conjoint creations of the imagination and the intellect. But the final acceptance or rejection of particular norms thus formulated is an activity of the higher will."

Though this book revolves around Babbitt's epistemologically relevant ideas, it also is a book about Ryn's own ideas as these correct, supplement, and heighten Babbitt's. For instance, Ryn draws attention to certain weaknesses and inconsistencies in Babbitt's relationship to modern aesthetics, and singles out for criticism Babbitt's insufficient appreciation of Benedetto Croce's important contribution to the notion of the creative imagination. Many of Croce's ideas, Ryn iterates, are similar to Babbitt's but are expressed with philosophical precision and systematic development that the American critic lacks. Ryn seeks, hence, to synthesize to advantage the ideas of Babbitt the dualist and those of Croce the monist—"to forge their respective strengths into a systematic whole, thus developing a new approach to the problem of knowledge." "Ideas contain potentialities for development," he goes on to say, "in sometimes unexpected directions."

Particularly helpful is Ryn's discussion of Babbitt's view of the role of the imagination as a source of wisdom and as a source of dangerous illusion. The "higher will" can, in this connection, be described as an "inner check," an expression of a kind of moral "uneasiness" (as Ryn expressively puts it)—that is, an instance of "the transcendent God breaking into consciousness…. It affords man opportunity to reconstitute his intentions." Ryn clarifies Babbitt's view of the moral function of art, the "moral imagination," which "imitates the universal" and gives us "an elevated sense of order, proportion and reality." In contrast, the "idyllic imagination" of Rousseau contributes to a distortion of our understanding of reality. Unlike Croce, as Ryn points out, Babbitt was to develop an insight about which professional philosophers (and, one could add, professional critics) know little or nothing: that "through the moral imagination man has an intuitive perception of the universal."

Ryn's judicious reading of Babbitt enables him to pinpoint a major cause of decline in Western society: "At the core of the decline he [Babbitt] sees a corruption of the imagination and with it moral character." It is certainly a pity that within the academy we do not have a larger number of critics who can read Babbitt and arrive at the discriminating judgments that Ryn conveys with a sense of urgency. (But, as Babbitt himself indicated, we should be grateful for the "keen-sighted few" among us!) The social-political consequences of "idyllic imagination," Ryn stresses, are there in any reluctance to have one's (un)real vision of the world tested—to see it in terms of historical reality or to subject a vision or idea to the analysis of reason: "Training of the moral imagination is thus inseparable from the training of moral character." The need to distinguish between falsehood and truth in the imagination never ceases, and only when we acknowledge this central principle with Babbitt and Ryn will we be able to grasp the eternal validity of first principles.

The examination of aesthetical and philosophical problems in Ryn's book is filled with challenge, though at the same time its pervasive theoretical concerns with aesthetics and philosophy in relation to Babbitt necessarily produce abstract considerations that must alert us to the aptness of F.R. Leavis's warning (in a famous exchange in 1937 with René Wellek) that literary criticism and philosophy are "quite distinct and different kinds of discipline."[5] Ryn's theoretical considerations have the effect at times of blurring Babbitt's identity as a literary critic and even dim the lucidity and the cogency of his critical expositions. Sometimes lost in Ryn's book is Babbitt's inimitable voice as a teacher, a great teacher—greater than a critic, as it is sometimes said. This voice is heard in an essay like "English and the Discipline of Ideas" (1920). The Babbitt of this essay is the Babbitt we need to hear more than ever; it is the Babbitt we forget at our peril, the Babbitt who is more fundamentally akin to *paideia* than to *epistēme*.

In this essay we hear the voice of the teacher and we gauge its tone, its rhythm, its toughness, and its intrinsic

humaneness. That voice must not be forgotten or trans-
formed, even as it must be restored to its true critical
primacy as it speaks to the problems of "literature and the
American college" and of "democracy and leadership." If
we are to derive the most value from Babbitt's public ministry of forty years, we must listen to what he has to say
about American society and culture. And what he has to say
attains its poignant representations in this essay:

> The issue…which must be faced squarely is whether our
> education, especially our higher education, is to be qual-
> itative and intensive or quantitative and extensive. Those
> who are filled with concern for the lot of humanity as a
> whole, especially for the less fortunate portions of it, are
> wont nowadays to call themselves idealists. We should at
> least recognize that ideals in this sense are not the same
> as standards and that they are often indeed the opposite
> of standards. If we are told that it is not democratic to
> produce the superior man, we should reply with
> Aristotle that the remedy for democracy is not more
> democracy, but that, on the contrary, if we wish a
> democracy that is to endure we should temper it with its
> opposite—with the idea of quality and selection.[6]

The Babbittian voice found in the preceding extracts is
the voice that must take precedence over any other voice
that is assigned to him. These extracts best reflect his
mind, his manner, and above all his "plain style." They have
the same effect and advantage of containing sound sense
under the weight of words, a quality that Babbitt shared
with an earlier man of letters, moralist, and critic, Samuel
Johnson. Like Dr. Johnson's, Babbitt's writing takes the
terse, vigorous tone of his talking as it emanates from the
rostrum in the lecture hall and as it inevitably relates to
"the vacuity of life." And that style conveys, unmistakably,
the concreteness, the masculine directness, the trans-

parency, and the sagacity that are characteristic of Babbitt as a man of letters always aware of his main critical responsibilities. Babbitt's words, as F. O. Matthiessen reminds us, "always bring us back to the phrase from Arnold he liked to quote: 'the imperious lonely thinking power.' He demonstrated in his own practice the cardinal importance for any civilization of a man's retaining his hold 'on the truths of the inner life.' In a period of prophets and confessors he refused to be either. He fulfilled the function of the critic, bleak though his isolation often was."[7]

The concrete reality of moral heroism in Babbitt the man of letters is registered in the civilized voice of the critic of literature, politics, and religion. Babbitt was a moralist through and through, believing as Arnold did that the struggle between the higher and the lower self is the essence of human life and can be understood dialectically in the light of "the imaginative reason." When studied in terms of its critico-philosophical and historico–textual essences, *Will, Imagination and Reason* should encourage its readers to conclude that if Americans could be made to listen to Babbitt's voice in its civilized and prophetic tone, our social and cultural situation would be manifestly better. It may very well be that Babbitt's influence today is not greater because there are certain overemphases in his so-called doctrine that becloud his true worth and hinder the unfolding of the true Babbitt. We must listen to his voice in its consistency and continuity before we venture to revaluate the texts it speaks of with cogency and lucidity. And until we do so Babbitt will continue to be perceived as something of an enigma in American intellectual and cultural history.

No American man of letters has equalled or surpassed either the maturity or the gravity of Babbitt's judgments, not even an Emerson, for precisely the reasons that More posits when he writes:

> He [Emerson] is preëminently the poet of religion and
> philosophy for the young; whereas men as they grow
> older are inclined to turn from him, in their more seri-
> ous needs, to those sages who have supplemented insight
> with a firmer grasp of the whole of human nature.[8]

The comparative connections that Ryn finds between
Babbitt and Croce underscore and turn our attention to
the sweep of Babbitt's vision. Other men of letters have
made singular contributions in the American scene, but
not with the kind of straightness and openness that Babbitt
displayed. He did not have the impishness of a John Jay
Chapman or the crankiness of an Edmund Wilson. He did
not have to flee from his native shores as did his greatest
student, T. S. Eliot, in order to mold his vision and find his
faith. He did not give in to the ambivalences and the ambi-
guities of a Lionel Trilling. He was a man of letters who,
robustly and tenaciously, personified Man thinking, and he
has not yet had a true successor.

For most Americans Babbitt's greatness remains too
great to fathom or bear, even as his integral Americanness
continues for the most part to perplex or irritate his countrymen. His writings have yet to become a bona fide part
of the American literary canon in the academy that now
sanctifies "prophets of extremity" like Foucault and
Derrida who breed the "purely insurrectionist attitude" (to
apply Babbitt's own prophetic phrase).

Babbitt's Americanness is distinguished not only on a
personal level of responsibility—his solidarity of character
and his burden of conscience as these identify his moral
discriminations—but also on a spiritual and intellectual
level—his sense of vocation and his moral earnestness in
diagnosing the American experience, its conditions, tensions, needs. Not to be overlooked is his steadiness of
purpose and his paradigmatic fortitude, for even as he
observed pernicious negatives, this schoolmaster of a

nation and good men did not capitulate to negations. He exemplifies "the making of the American mind" in the very framework of universal history itself as a part of noetic life. Anyone who examines, say, an essay like "The Critic and American Life" will appreciate precisely those values and universals that Babbitt seeks to bring to bear on the quality of general critical intelligence in its American ambience. The whole circle of his ideas, surely, is present in these two sentences from that essay: "The serious critic is more concerned with achieving a correct scale of values and so seeing things proportionately than with self-expression. His essential virtue is poise."[9]

Increasingly the humanistic standards of discipline, decorum, and duty that Babbitt espoused, the moral law of cause and effect that he esteemed, and the courage of judgment that he exemplified are fatalities of disorder and decadence. Babbitt's Americanness remains essentially homeless in an age in which an arrogant orthodoxy of enlightenment not only proscribes first principles but also demands that, as Eliot puts it, "we conceal from ourselves the unpleasant knowledge of the real values by which we live." With Claes G. Ryn, a gifted and responsible celebrator of the legacy of our greatest American man of letters in modern times, we must continue to work for Irving Babbitt's homecoming.

## II

Like Claes Ryn, Milton Hindus continues the work for Babbitt's final homecoming and, in effect, further testifies to the widening of the circle of Babbitt's readers and commentators. His book on *Irving Babbitt, Literature, and the Democratic Culture* (1994) illustrates, too, how a keen understanding of Irving Babbitt's writings makes one an even better critic. One can only hope, even if such hope is small at the present precipitous stage of American civilization, that present-day students and teachers of humane letters are exposed not only to Babbitt's ideas and beliefs, but also to his gifted interpreters. Babbitt is an American man of letters who exerts good influence and has enduring value for those who, like Professor Hindus, read him seriously and who examine his achievement intelligently. That is all, really, that Babbitt himself would have asked from his readers and auditors. In him, in his work, measure and humility were virtues that illuminated his views of life, literature, and thought. Hindus's essays, as collected and presented in this book, convey these virtues and also assimilate them. Though his essays, in the main, are about Babbitt, they are ultimately essays that keenly display Hindus's own autonomy and integrity as a critic. They remind us that the critical spirit, when and if it truly absorbs the greatness and excellence given generously by a major critic like Babbitt, can attain both latitude and depth—and enduring beneficence. The need for exemplars is today more urgent than ever, if we are not to become captives of the destructive habits that afflict American intellectual life in general and the critical function in particular. "No one more faithfully continues Babbitt's task than Milton Hindus," writes Russell Kirk in the introduction.

Half of the essays here are about Babbitt, but Babbitt's

ethical precepts are the shaping spirit of the other half of Hindus's essays on literature and democratic culture found here. That Babbitt's ideas have lasting value, and that his influence survives in spite of the nihilisms that stalk the academy, are amply and thankfully evident in Hindus's book. To be sure, Babbitt's ideas and influence are hardly welcomed in the American intelligentsia community, or in the general periodicals, or in the world of higher learning (about which Babbitt wrote with deep insight in a book still in print and worth study and reflection, *Literature and the American College*). But that, in the past two decades, a growing number of books by and about Babbitt have been published and command respect, underscores the perseverance and the vigor of a minority critical movement in the United States. The following books particularly stand out: Thomas R. Nevin's *Irving Babbitt: An Intellectual Study* (1984), an illuminating discussion of Babbitt's mind, historical background, and humanistic formulations; Stephen C. Brennan and Stephen R. Yarbrough's *Irving Babbitt* (1987), an able and concise introduction to Babbitt's work and thought; and J. David Hoeveler's *The New Humanism: A Critique of Modern America, 1990-1940* (1977), a discerning analysis of the collective thought of the New Humanists. This movement, or remnant, points to the need to oppose the intellectual and critical totalitarianism that now takes us even further down "the road to serfdom."

Here, then, Hindus testifies to those properties of the critical pursuit that Babbitt was to honor and exemplify in his teachings and writings: moral responsibility, seriousness, discrimination, discipline, order. For Hindus, no less than Babbitt, the critical function is inescapably tied to the ethical character of man and the character of civilization— and to the political, economic, philosophical, educational, and religious interrelationships that necessarily define and mold character in its whole and in its parts, and at all levels of civilized life. And for Hindus, no less than Babbitt, the final test of the critic is that of distinguishing between "the wisdom of the age," with its flux, transience, corruption, and the wisdom of the ages, as it emerges from historical experience in the individuating forms of "tradition as history" and "tradition as heritage."

The essays directly elucidating Babbitt's achievement are invariably helpful to a reader, and make unmistakably clear why his work speaks to our condition. Throughout Hindus emphasizes Babbitt's central concern, the problem of conduct as it is inextricably tied to convictions and principles. For Babbitt, what distinguishes man from thing is the human capacity to exert interior discipline and, in effect, to implement the classical qualities of decorum, proportion, restraint, and measure as these are translated into the inner check. The disciplinary element inherent in these qualities, as Hindus stresses, is what guards against the anarchic freedom and the license of the emotions that Jean-Jacques Rousseau glorified and that modernism enshrines *ad absurdum*. Babbitt, in short, affirmed the confluence of standards of the inner self and standards of the commonwealth.

In his essays on Babbitt, as Russell Kirk notes, "Milton Hindus opens our eyes to a great conservative man of letters." Thus, whether Hindus is assessing Babbitt's *Rousseau and Romanticism, The Masters of Modern French Criticism, Democracy and Leadership,* or Babbitt's translation of *The Dhammapada*, he provides one with generous critical directions that one does not meet in contemporary critical movements that breed confusion and disorder. Centrality, not dissipation, is the benchmark of Babbitt's contribution and meaning, and in underscoring this fact Hindus registers minority dissent that has the capacity to restore to the critical function its basic purpose to distinguish and to pass judgment upon literary works, separating true art from false art. Refusal to recognize the validity of this view of criticism, Hindus reminds us in his essays, leads to the mediocrity that now assumes forms of decadence in both imaginative literature and literary criticism.

Evangels of the new social order, of the new age and the new morality, have steadily, and arrogantly, chosen to live in a modern dreamworld with its unchecked ideologies, chimeras, fantasies, reveries, utopias that plunge us deeper and deeper in a vacuum of disinheritance and that "dark night of the mind," of which Richard Weaver speaks. The dream, the nightmare, is never absent; it captivates mind, body, and soul; and it becomes the mainstay of our technicism in all of its manifestations and empty optimisms. It is a dream, as Babbitt would say, that categorically separates one from "the immediate data of consciousness." The "terrible simplifiers" who infest the American mind and soul, and who dictate taste and sensibility, unfailing sanctify this dream, cruelly rent from the realities that Babbitt wants us neither to ignore nor yet to despair of, but to grapple with strenuously and positively.

Reading Hindus on Babbitt prompts the thought here that no American statesman, teacher, or philosopher—no American holding a position of leadership—should consider himself, or herself, truly educated, and, yes, truly enlightened, who has not studied *Democracy and Leadership*. Such a reading could even inaugurate, correctively, the beginning of the inner check that both leaders and polity sorely need if the nightmare that Babbitt warns against is not to become absolute, the irreversible "abolition of man." Babbitt's writings, Hindus rightly demonstrates, hold paramount moral and spiritual lessons for all generations, modern and postmodern.

Hindus's essays not directly relating to Babbitt nevertheless deal with subjects that long preoccupied the latter as teacher and critic: American society, culture, politics, education, literature. For the reader these essays are much rewarding in terms of critical commentary and judgment.

Indeed, there is in these particular essays a double critical, and catechetical, value, as the reader derives from Hindus's explorations and scrutinies insights into contemporary problems, and also the additional benefit of Babbitt's steady influence. There is an inclusive and defining solidity of critical thinking here that coalesces with an older critic's effect on his critical heritor. A line of continuity emerges in enriching and enlightening ways, reminding us of the truth of Babbitt's contention that "there is always the unity at the heart of change." Indeed, we are equally reminded here that when there is no continuity, no centrality, no abiding principles, no ethos, the result is disconnection and, in effect, the destructiveness that now passes for critical thought in the academy.

Hindus does not choose to ignore the paradigms of an older criticism, that is, a great predecessor's enduring worth. He is a critical practitioner who knows the full and continuing value of the virtue of loyalty that a regnant "orthodoxy of enlightenment" outlaws and persecutes, to the peril of American society and culture. He does not seek, in other words, to declare his independence at the cost of rootlessness. The critic's loyalty to an American father of criticism transforms into a transcendent sense of responsibility, forged as it is in the ongoing crisis of modernity. In this respect Hindus's critical metaphysic has the kind of ontological validity and relevance that resides in the need for "roots of order"—and also in "visions of order." Surely those who scorn the constituents of this critical metaphysic invite catastrophism.

Following Babbitt, Hindus speaks for a point of view that, however unpopular, refuses to bow down before "men deep in Utopian Speculations," a phrase that Hindus quotes from the *Federalist Papers,* which he associates with the qualities of wisdom, moderation, humility. In remarking on "the future of democracy in the United States," Hindus stresses: "We are in no particular need of reform again, or reconstruction, or dreams of perfection designed to make the mechanism of government more responsive to a restless desire for change." And in examining "literature and the democratic culture," he affirms the need of standards in order both to judge and to save literature from sophistic and gnostic deformations.

In looking at the autobiographies of three American presidents—Martin Van Buren's (as published in volume 2 of *The Proceedings of the American Historical Association* for the year 1918); Ronald Reagan's *Where's the Rest of Me?* (1965); and George Bush's *Looking Forward* (1987)—Hindus singles out the qualities of responsibility, restraint, and humility which he finds missing from the "more imperious, charismatic personages who have occupied the presidency since." It is refreshing, in this respect, to find here a critic who ultimately views criticism as the pursuit of virtue—a view that contemporary critics disdain. Hindus focuses on transcendent standards of character in his critiques of these autobiographies in particular, and of art in general; he refuses to be fooled by sham values, and claims, as well as by pseudo-art and pseudo-criticism. To emphasize standards of character, as does Hindus, requires fortitude, especially in a time of history when character and the moral virtues are deemed meaningless and valueless.

Hindus is a brave exception to an inordinate number of American critics who remain imprisoned in a sheer relativism that falls into anarchy. "America...seems to be subject to the strong pull of its fantastic and overheated imagination," Hindus warns, "which suggests that nothing is impossible, that history is bunk and can be safely ignored, and that there are no limits to human potential. When such fantasy threatens to part us from the ground of reality, strong cables are necessary to hold it down." The failure to heed this warning has grave consequences, which are everywhere apparent in American civilization. Of course, our leaders at all levels believe they are cognizant of these consequences, especially in the world of education. But their solutions are those of "social perfectionists" whose faith in the religion of illusion is unbending. "Deformed ideologies," to quote Eric Voegelin's phrase, increasingly fuel this religion, and put huge obstacles in the way of those who will not embrace it. Still, the future does not, cannot, belong to new "sophisters, economists, and calculators." For as long as there are critics who possess "force of character," the legacy of Irving Babbitt, to which Milton Hindus, no less than Claes Ryn, gives witness, preserves "the living principle."

## CHAPTER SEVEN

# An Act of Reparation

## I

Irving Babbitt never wavered in what he viewed as being his commanding office as a teacher and critic. During the more than forty years of his career he held firmly to a position, both avoiding and scorning "sudden conversions" and "pistol-shot transformations." He never fell into the traps of confusion and expediency; nor did he ever compromise his position either out of self-doubt or of self-interest. His critical position, as hard and tough as it was sincere and authentic, sanctioned neither retreat nor re-routing. Even as storms of controversy (and abuse) raged around him he did not give way. He was, in his special style, a battler; "never say die," in the best tradition of that worn phrase, could have easily been one of his slogans. To claim, as is the habit of some commentators, that Babbitt is monolithic as a critical thinker is to subtract from the real truth and worth of his achievement. It is to perpetuate, in fact, the myth that his enemies came to create about his being a reactionary. His position was, to be sure, four-square, but it was also a position that excelled in character; he never betrayed his conscience, the truths of which, once he had discovered them, he possessed irretrievably. In the academic world, where one too often finds all kinds of weasels and upstarts, Babbitt proved himself to be a great and brave man. He had guts.

This tenacity of character and principle is compellingly present in Babbitt's creed of the New Humanism. Unfortunately his position has generally been misunderstood and misrepresented. His enemies gave it too little credit and his sympathizers expected too much from it. Babbitt himself defined his creed clearly, augmented considerably by the simplicity of his delineation of his ideas and judgments. "Unprofitable subtleties," conundrums, complexities, and paradoxes never interfered with or distorted Babbitt's presentation of his creed. Its other most notable quality is its centripetal force. His vision of order is impelled by his principle of control. In this respect, Babbitt's position was to militate against anything that leads one to fantasy or illusion. Limits, not expansion, is an informing word in his concepts.

It could be said that the restrictive essences of Babbitt's thought worked against its popular acceptance and influence, in much the same way that the human capacity for reconstructive change, or what Babbitt termed a "metaphysic of the many," as preached by his famous contemporary, the philosopher John Dewey, spurred on an epidemic scale a refashioning of thought not only in philosophy but also in law, in education, in politics. A "maker of twentieth-century America," Dewey appealed to man's expansionist impulse. His radical optimism, in the contexts and with the specifics of an inclusive program of social action, was appropriate to a national mood and a liberal trend. Human possibilities unlimited: to this doctrine of change and growth, in the attainment of creative, that is, pragmatic, "consummations," Dewey gave his first and last loyalty, as even this one sentence from his voluminous writings shows: "Democracy is the faith that the process of experience is more important than any special result attained, so that special results achieved are of ultimate value only as they are used to enrich and order the ongoing process." Any emphasis, then, on inner, or spiritual life, as watched over by a purgative and humbling "inner check," as made by Babbitt, could hardly compete with Dewey's view of life as an evolving social experience of "shared good."

Babbitt's humanistic doctrine is ultimately character-ized not by ambition but by humility with its intrinsic, its total and irrevocable sense of man's limit-situation and, consequently, of man's need for self-discipline and self-reliance. There is nothing either programmatic or enthusiastic about Babbitt's doctrine; indeed, it is austere and even solitary, lacking any grand temporal plans or metaphysical promises of redemption. It is a doctrine com-pletely shorn of personal or collective illusions and non-essentials: the dreams of infinitude, of a "great society" and of a "city of God" alike, are for Babbitt vague and unre-alizable. One could say in this respect that Babbitt's doctrine is *spiritual,* as this word conjoins ethical and moral constituents, rather than religious in a supernatural sense. It revolves around conscience rather than grace. His innately Protestant sensibility is severely schooled by his classicist and Orientalist metaphysic in its assimilated forms and consecration to what Babbitt termed "the ser-vice of a high, impersonal reason." For Babbitt reason is an indwelling and salutary force of mediation, legislating restraint and proportion,—the middle way, the law of measure, that avoids the extremes of human consciousness, whether as an Augustinian curse *of* or as a Rousseauistic adventure *in* consciousness. Babbitt was a genuine ecu-menist. His humanism, to repeat, was a finely wrought reconciliation of East and West, of Confucius and Aristotle, of Buddha and Christ.

Both his friendly and his enemy critics have failed to appreciate the simple and direct meaning of Babbitt's doc-trine. For T. S. Eliot, it was inadequately religious, an alternative or ancillary doctrine that suppressed the divine or outrightly denied the revelation of the supernatural. For Edmund Wilson it was insufferably reactionary, a doctrine containing "not really conclusions from evidence, but the mere unexamined prejudices of a bigoted Puritan heritage." The point is that Babbitt's teachings failed to pass the "ultimate" tests of Orthodoxy or of Enlightenment and, as a result, were never given a fair hearing. Babbitt himself would rightly dismiss the charges of his enemy critics as a hodge-podge of humanitarian, utilitarian, and sentimental opinions, invariably failing to adhere to some higher principle of unity, or standard, with which to measure mere manifoldness and change or a mere multiplicity of a scale of values.

That his greatest pupil, T. S. Eliot, and eventually even his closest ally, Paul Elmer More, chose to deprecate the spiritual dimension of Babbitt's doctrine must be noted as an unfortunate phenomenon. Babbitt, after all, was not a theologian. He was, however, a humanistic teacher and prophetic critic of extraordinary ability, as time and history have proved. "On being human," to use the title of a volume of one of More's *New Shelburne Essays,* and on being human in an age discrediting the older dualism, underlined Babbitt's prophetic concern. This concern is at the very center of his mission; it is a total concern as it relates to an ongoing interaction of economic, political, philosophical, religious, and educational problems in the modern world. No two passages from Babbitt's texts better catch his significance as an ethical prophet of modernism, in whose words the invisible God becomes audible, than the following, the first written at the beginning of his career, the second at the end:

> The greatest of vices according to Buddha is the lazy yielding to the impulses of temperament *(pamāda);* the greatest virtue *(appamāda)* is the opposite of this, the awakening from the sloth and lethargy of the senses, the

constant exercise of the active will. The last words of the dying Buddha to his disciples was an exhortation to practice this virtue unremittingly *(appāmadena sampādetha)*.

He [Buddha] has succeeded in compressing the wisdom of the ages into a sentence: "To refrain from all evil, to achieve the good, to purify one's heart, this is the teaching of the Awakened." The Buddhist commentary is interesting: When you repeat the words, they seem to mean nothing, but when you try to put them into practice, you find they mean everything.

## II

Now whether or not Babbitt is, say, a philosopher, or an aesthetician, or a literary critic, or a moral agent, or a social commentator, or a conservative ideologue, or a guru is a debate that, at least among academic boulevardiers, is fated to go on. No less evident, though more alarming and revealing in its constancy and consistency, is the violent tone that marks this debate, sometimes as violent when it appears today as it was in the twenties and thirties when the New Humanism, with Babbitt as its chief spokesman, enjoyed something of a vogue. In any case, identifying the nature of Babbitt's work and thought—his mission—is not difficult. If one must insist, however, on pinning some kind of name-tag on Babbitt before admitting him into some grove of academe, and certainly before considering the significance of his contribution (though it is much more than that simplistic word could ever indicate), not one but several name-tags can be presented. Generalist, diagnostician, teacher, thinker: in each of these categories Babbitt acquitted himself honestly, honorably, humbly.

That, as Austin Warren believes, Babbitt can be counted among the "New England Saints" is perhaps a claim that, in the end, transcends all others and makes them finally superfluous. For some, no doubt, Warren's claim may be extravagant, even as for Babbitt, who insisted on basing all judgments on the "immediate data of consciousness," it may have been found embarrassing. A mediating designation that identifies Babbitt, and one that, it is to be hoped, neither he nor his enemies would quibble over, is catechist, the office of the catechist defined as being that of not only instructing and teaching but also examining. Indeed, Babbitt's teachings and writings (and the latter are the fruit of the former) disclose precisely his catechistical style and approach, as well as his duty, which was his act of faith. Only when Babbitt is seen in this refining light will proper recognition of his achievement be possible. Only, that is, when he is seen as a teacher in the old, and catechistical, sense will he be revered in the sense that a Ralph Waldo Emerson is revered. Clearly, in the case of Babbitt, any plea for critical reconsideration must also predicate what is even more important, a categorical act of reparation.

The prospects for a full-scale reparation are not too good in the present derelict phase of American culture. It is a phase in which post-liberal and now post-modern driftings and shiftings are everywhere in abundance, and with an abundance of frightening consequences, which Babbitt himself had prophesied. If we can boast with all our indiscriminating liberal optimism of being a nation of the "New Adam," we are hardly a nation of catechumens. The catecheses of Irving Babbitt are no more to the liking of most Americans than any message that stresses moral or spiritual restraint of any sort. "Outward bound," the bigger the better, not the "inner check," characterizes the yearnings of most Americans today. Early on in his life Babbitt, a brave man, chose to resist this centrifugal quest, equating it with an imperialism as dangerous in its psychic as in its social-political dimensions.

It is sometimes said by some of Babbitt's Harvard pupils that at the close of his life he grew pessimistic as to the efficacy of his mission. Such a feeling would be natural to any sensitive and intelligent observer of the chaos of values embracing the whole of modern life. Indeed, no modern American thinker exposed himself more to attack than Babbitt. From T. V. Smith to, in a virulent letter appearing in *The American Scholar,* Ernest Earnest, the attacks have continued with the kind of intolerance that prompted Douglas Bush to protest against the unqualified charges aimed at Babbitt by "automatic liberals who," he notes, "can be as intolerant of nonconformity as automatic conservatives." "Nonconformity" may seem the wrong word to use to describe Babbitt's thought. But when one deliberates on the matter and considers the power of the reigning orthodoxy of enlightenment then one can easily see that Babbitt's catechistical thought, positing as it does the idea of a minority culture, goes against the grain. The fact remains that many Americans are by now so addicted to the illusion of liberalism, with all its promises of a "fair deal," that they can hardly be patient when confronted with the demands—and Babbitt never ceased making them—for affirming the moral constant and the moral imperative. No, it is not easy, in the peculiar circumstances surrounding Babbitt, to make an act of reparation.

Needless to say, we should be thankful not only for a widening of the circle of Babbitt's readers, but also for the reissuing of some of his books. But a kindling of interest in Babbitt does not necessarily mean that his moral and ethical ideas have gained a commanding presence in the intellectual community or in the social-political realm. Renewed interest in Babbitt does not necessarily signify either the acceptance or the implementation of his teachings, especially in the groves of academe. The hard fact remains that Babbitt's value to us, if it is to survive in a dynamic form, will be ultimately determined by the efforts of what Professor Stephen Tonsor calls a "creative conservative minority," which generally stands outside the centers of power. The fate of Babbitt's achievement will, then, depend on how a creative minority preserves and advances his worth and relevance. This particular task is, in the end, part of the larger civilizational task which Tonsor identifies in these reminding words: "A new creative minority must attempt...to make explicit all that is implicit in the past, to bring into actuality all that a previous generation posited only in potentiality."[1]

Clearly Babbitt's writings incorporate, in a very masculine, sometimes racy and aphoristic style, his teachings, again underlining the catechistical quality of his work and thought. Of writings that are teachings, as in Babbitt's case, we have immense corrective need, particularly when these are filled with insight and wisdom. Any return to and refrequentation of sapiential literature can have both therapeutic and antidotal value. There are at least two major problems, however, to be overcome in encouraging readers to return to Babbitt's works. First, from a pedagogical point of view, there are no longer any "required texts" at any educational level, so that, for example, a J.R.R. Tolkien is counted equal to Joseph Conrad and a Samuel Beckett to Shakespeare. And second, most persons, including and even especially those who have had a college or university education, have never read the right books, the right poets and novelists, and the right critics and thinkers.

What we see in this phenomenon, as symptom and portent, is the cruel absence of a great tradition, sacrificed, obviously, to the changing climate of opinion that goes hand-in-hand with cultural pluralism and diversity. To judge by the way contemporary civilization is going we can have only moderate expectations of any effort to revive Babbitt's relevance to the modern situation. But as

in any permanent doctrine that revolves around first principles our expectations must themselves be accompanied
and judged by unequivocal criteria. Any effort to renew
connection with Babbitt's work, in part or in whole,
should be counted a worthy one. "To be understood by a
few intelligent people," observes T. S. Eliot, "is all the
influence a man requires."

## III

In Babbitt we observe a judging mind hard at work, and
it is precisely this process that marks him as a modern
profoundly aware of the disequilibrium affecting every
aspect of civilization since the Renaissance. He connected
this disequilibrium with man's expansive desires and with
naturalistic trends, particularly as embodied in Rousseau's
thought. To combat these conditions of existence he chose
an active ministry of life, what he called a positive and critical humanism. Hence, he was to be concerned, as he
insisted, not so much with meditation, the culmination of
true religion, as with mediation, or the law of measure
governing man in his secular relations. He is finally to be
seen, then, as a sapiential and a prophetic critic: as one
who seeks to teach the meaning of wisdom, stressing,
above all, the priority of self-reform over social reform,
and who warns of the dire consequences, for man and society, when standards, containing a center of judgment, are
not maintained.

In this critical role Babbitt was to raise questions of a
humanistic rather than an eschatological nature. His primary concern was with life and with the destiny of man
rather than with faith and redemption. He himself admitted, in fact, that he did side with the naturalists in rejecting
outside authority in favor of the immediate and the expe-

riential. But for Babbitt, as a critic relying on psychological analysis supported by a growing body of evidence, his answers to questions regarding the moral and ethical life were to be radically different, and different in a tempering way. That is, he believed that, with Rousseau, the naturalists asked the right questions but gave the wrong answers. In short, Babbitt sought to show the unsoundness of answers manufactured in the liberal and democratizing contexts of "relativity" and of "the progress and service of humanity." He found in their answers (and in their time) not only a reliance on a crass materialism but also, and more importantly, a sham spirituality. He had, first and always, the unhappy and unpopular task of indicting the extremes and the excrescences of the epoch in which we are still living, at once proffering and defending the disciplining exercises of "the veto power."

The dialectical essences of this task are nowhere more advantageously or vigorously displayed than in *Democracy and Leadership*. First published in 1924, but long out-of-print, it has been reissued as an inexpensive and handsome Liberty Classic.[2] One must hope that, as far as it is possible to do so in an age of lust and grab, and of cowardice and betrayal, this reprinting of a book so long confined to ignominy initiates an act of reparation. It gives one even the smallest hope that the battle that Babbitt waged was not in vain, that it is still being waged, even if necessarily in the underground by a small band of beleaguered humanistic loyalists. As a compendium of his ideas, values, and judgments, *Democracy and Leadership* is Babbitt's most spiritually strenuous work. In it, beginnings and endings, first principles and last principles, conjoin and cohere.

If *Democracy and Leadership* can be said to be Babbitt's catechesis, it can also be said to be his *stromata,* the bedrock of his critical teachings. It is a brave and honest book, written by a saint who is as tough as a saint ought to be. It is not a book for small minds, or for spiritual loafers. Nor is it a book for the ego-ridden or -poisoned, neither for "little Napoleons" nor for academic pundits and dry-as-dust pedants bloated with their self-importance, with what Babbitt calls "man's expansive conceit." It is, in a very vital way, an homiletic book of ethical and moral discourse that gives a positive basis to humility; a book to be read continuously, catechetically, pondered and meditated on, assimilated and synthesized—and, as Babbitt would want it, lived. It is a great book, a great critical vision, "a supreme act of analysis" that traces causes and effects and distinguishes between things which are at the center different.

*Democracy and Leadership* is in some ways a misnomer, for it is much more than just a study in social science and politics. All categories and conditions of human existence, in their interrelations and interdependence, are examined here with critical ferocity. Babbitt is unsparing in citing errors (*e.g.,* relativity, humanitarianism, naturalism) that lead to indiscipline and in turn to breakdown, whether in private life or in public. Throughout his diagnosis concentrates on facts, precisely on those "facts" that Rousseau and his followers insisted on setting aside: the discarding of standards and the experience of the past; the growing evils of unlimited democracy and the eradication of the aristocratic principle; the excesses of the "idyllic imagination" as it supplants "moral imagination"; the establishment of a "civil religion," with all of its secular and material aggrandizements, and the concomitant diminution of both a hierarchy of values and of the centripetal elements in life; the substitution of the doctrine of natural goodness for the older doctrine of man's sinfulness and fallibility; the confusion of mechanical and material progress with moral progress. The political situation, thus, is viewed, defined, and characterized in its ethical and moral contexts.

Babbitt is unfailing in stressing that the lack in life of a reverence for some unifying center, or oneness, has its ancillary counterpart in man's "expansive conceit" (instanced as divers forms of "imperialism": aggressive intellect, as well as aggressive will to power—the *libido dominandi*—rejecting all forms of control). It is the decline of the inner life, of inner vision, as the voice of conscience and as the possessor of spiritual truth, that Babbitt focuses on inasmuch as public life reflects inner life. It is in the end, he keeps reminding us, a matter of perceiving and affirming the idea of value as it restrains "the cheap and noisy tendencies of the passing hour." Once this transcending and inclusive humanistic idea of value is negated, in any degree or part, the whole fabric of life is rent. For Babbitt, in this respect, the modern political movement signals a battle between the spirit of Rousseau, espousing the "law of the members," and the spirit of Edmund Burke, affirming the "law of the spirit." Appropriately, Babbitt uses as an epigraph to *Democracy and Leadership* these words, summarizing by centralizing, from Burke's *Letter to a Member of the National Assembly:*

> Society cannot exist unless a controlling power upon will and appetite be placed somewhere, and the less of it there is within, the more there must be without. It is ordained in the eternal constitution of things, that men of intemperate minds cannot be free.

In the modern movement of democracy Babbitt sees not "a democracy of elevation," as Russell Kirk expresses it, but rather an unbridled political expression of naturalism that frequently results in "decadent imperialism." There is not only an absence of standards, as Babbitt shows in his final and most profound chapter, "Democracy and Standards." The consequences of such a situation are far-reaching and damaging. The majoritarian ethos, or what he terms a "divine average," is incapable of effecting standards of discrimination. The critical process of selection or rejection is sacrificed to a utilitarian-sentimental conception of life, to what he speaks of elsewhere as "eleutheromania." Yet what this conception fails to recognize, Babbitt stresses, and here he helps considerably to distinguish between the positions of the "true and false liberals," is the constant need for ethical effort, in all of its disciplining and integrating forms.

To resist the centrifugal tendencies of a democracy that transposes into a dreamland, as elusive as it is illusory, Babbitt notes the related and additional need of restoring the moral struggle to the individual: the recovery in some form of "the civil war in the cave." Substituting sentiment for conscience and expansive emotion for the inner life epitomizes for Babbitt the evils of an unlimited democracy that flouts the aristocratic principle, which he associates with the traditional forms of discipline, with the "inner check,"—with, in a word, *character.* "The unit to which all things must finally be referred," he maintains, "is not the State or humanity or any other abstraction, but the man of character. Compared with this ultimate human reality, every other reality is only a shadow in the mist." These were, and are, brave words that we do not now even hear from preachers in the pulpit, preferring as we do to hear about "the power of positive thinking," still another form of utilitarian-sentimental self-deception advanced by religious and political leaders alike. Indeed, the problem of leadership was for Babbitt the major moral problem in an age whose "empire of chimeras" he steadfastly countered with an altogether understandable prophetic disdain.

*Democracy and Leadership* discloses the austere and rigorous workings not merely of a "conservative mind" but of a "universal mind," always speaking directly, and with courage of judgment, to a specific problem—"to the distinction...between a sound and an unsound individualism." In Babbitt's language to be sure, it is the blows of a hammer that we hear, rather than that which, as Shakespeare tells us, "gives us more palm in beauty than we have." Babbitt, a critic of integrity, wore no masks, had no pretensions or poses as "man and teacher," refused (as he said) to "put on sympathy a burden that it cannot bear," allowed nothing to muddle the keen inspection of facts. The pitiless facts of human history and experience (regardless of any claims for the "goodness of heart" as a substitute for moral obligations), he maintained, were incontrovertible: "What man needs, if we are to believe the Lord's prayer, is bread and wisdom. What man, at least Roman man, wanted, about the time that prayer was uttered, was bread and the circus."

Babbitt chose to describe himself as a "moral realist," going on with emphatic forthrightness to add: "If the moral realist seems hard to the idealist, this is because of his refusal to shift, in the name of sympathy or social justice or on any other ground, the struggle between good and evil from the individual to society."

However heavy the burden of his troubling responsibility, Babbitt did not succumb to world-weariness; he did not repudiate the value of spiritual effort. To be sure, he viewed the future with apprehension. "The latter stages of the naturalistic dissolution of civilization with which we are menaced are," he wrote, "thanks to scientific 'progress,' likely to be marked by incidents of almost inconceivable horror." With force of insight and with ethical and moral gravamen, he wrestled with those fundamental life-questions that relate to the fate of man in the modern world. What he chose to say about this world of increasing material organization combined with an ever-growing spiritual anarchy ("power without wisdom"), and about the need for a search for a remedy, continues to make Babbitt's work and thought disturbing and unpalatable. What modern man has chosen to listen to—one that makes for easy listening and easy living—is the doctrine of John Dewey, which, whatever its philosophical authority, as Eliseo Vivas has reminded us, prevents the development of piety and fails to stress nobility and dignity. Babbitt was fully aware of the braying voice of the world, but he bore his witness bravely, uncomplainingly.

## IV

"In the long run democracy will be judged," Babbitt writes in *Democracy and Leadership*, "no less than other forms of government, by the quality of its leaders, a quality that will depend in turn on the quality of their vision." Babbitt's words should remind us that the need for leadership, always urgent, remains ever more urgent in our time. We have reached a stage in history when the socio-political crisis of leadership goes hand-in-hand with what might be called the spiritual crisis of nihilism: that ultimate negation of moral principles of order and belief. In many ways this twin crisis is the off-shoot of what Jacob Burckhardt was to speak of, with particular reference to the French Revolution, as the "authorization to perpetual revision." In American society and culture, especially since the end of World War II, but going on throughout the twentieth century, we have seen an incessant revision of standards of leadership, as well as of American civilization itself, as leadership at all levels of national life has taken on specious forms.

Increasingly we have discarded standards of leadership that make for greatness and for that vision without which a civilization perishes. It is all too evident that many Americans do not relate confidently to the qualities that typify a great leader, one who, in Burckhardt's words, "is the man of exceptional intellectual or moral power whose activity is directed to a general aim, that is, a whole nation, a whole civilization, humanity itself." These are noble words, to be sure, and portray the noble aims of those who have "greatness of soul." Burckhardt, of course, does not permit idealism to overshadow hard facts, hard realities, and he cautions us by emphasizing that the idea of greatness, both as benefactor and as beneficence, has intrinsic ambiguity, if not relativeness. "Greatness is all that we are not," he emphasizes, if only to warn us that to find exemplary leadership is often problematic. We must always be prepared for disappointment and disillusionment in our search for a leader, given the human condition. In the present time, when the lures of mediocrity inform human aspirations, as well as concepts of leadership, the *desiderata* that Burckhardt associates with great leaders merit close attention. Growing wings to overcome gravity, to evoke Plato's wondrous image, is, or should be, a continual goal. Human culture and character advance, creatively and critically, only insofar as ascent is our purpose and effort. "Who shall ascend the hill of the Lord?" is an eternal question that the Psalmist asks of Man.

We must not allow ourselves to be misled by "terrible simplifiers" who would reduce human life and achievement to the lowest common denominator, even as we now see and experience the baleful results of this phenomenon in all facets of contemporary life. At the point when we no longer proclaim qualitative standards, subordinating them to socio-political agenda and expediency, we sink into the trough of mediocrity. If we are to avoid the awful costs of such a descendancy, we must, however unpopular and vulnerable our position may be, insist that standards of achievement, of life, of discrimination, should determine our range of awareness. If, too, we are not to be subsumed by the anthill of modern life, we must maintain at a maximal point a keen awareness of excellence, of criteria, of obligations—of greatness. Above all we must insist, with Babbitt, on those qualities of leadership that measure not so much practical success but rather the capacity for growth of insight and wisdom in terms of the moral life and the ethical life. To adopt a policy of silence or of neglect with regard to the higher metaphysical attributes of leadership, or to convert these attributes into exclusively equalitarian demands, and fallacies, trivializes the meaning of leadership. When and where standards are ignored, or scorned, or silenced, the consequences are injurious to civilization, to the polity, to governance. A morally impoverished society will produce morally impoverished leaders. Either we strive to strengthen leadership or we proceed to trivialize the very nature of its responsibility, if not its *raison d'être*.

In whom do we now recognize and salute leaderly qualities? Who are representative of great leadership? What accounts for the growing diminution of standards of leadership, of "men of light and leading" who, for Edmund Burke, combine "a disposition to preserve, and an ability to improve"? One who dares to answer these questions in the light of current practices and habits is bound to notice both a general drifting of leadership and a shifting of standards. The process of deterioration and debasement, once begun, is difficult to arrest, particularly in a technologico-Benthamite society that respects neither moral determinants nor moral deterrents. Such a nullifying process is registered in the ways in which men and women today judge the nature, the mission and ethos, of leadership, and of leaders who are unfriendly to the venerable triad of reason, Scripture, and tradition. With the growing absence of standards and discipline of leadership one can also observe a commensurate absence of leaders capable of guiding the citizenry to a higher moral and in turn socio-political ground. As such, leadership itself is annexed by the marketplace; it becomes its handmaiden and accomplice, complying with the prevailing climate of opinion and adapting itself to the whirl of the world. The idea of and the needs for leadership are thus reduced to a quantitative state, to a kind of emptiness, even entropy.

A tyranny of "quantitative reductionism," as Father Stanley Jaki uses that term, afflicts an entire society and culture and conduces decay at all levels of life. Leadership itself, both as concept and as need, undergoes transmutation once the forces of reductionism take hold. The transcendent purpose and meaning of leadership are made relative as standards and expectations are minimized or scuttled. Clearly, the eclipse of the idea of excellence is directly reflected in the eclipse of the quality of leaders— and, too, of a people's perception of representatives of leadership. This perception increasingly becomes a decadent one that cruelly excludes those canons of leadership that identify Ortega y Gasset's "select man" of magnanimous words and work. Today our "representative men" inevitably mirror the consequences of "authorization to perpetual revisionism," hostile to centrality, principle, discrimination, as well as to both the historical and the moral sense that provide the prudence and the virtue that restrict the force of barbarism. "Barbarism," Ortega reminds us, "is the absence of norms and of any possible appeal based on them."

Leadership that succumbs to "the absence of norms" in effect admits to a failure of nerve, the results of which are everywhere in evidence, as sham leaders come forth to fill the void. Still, the search for leadership does go on, but at lesser, surrogate levels. In a society in which qualities of leadership have receded and leaders exert no deep appeal to the heart, mind, and soul of the citizenry, the consequential vacuum must be filled to compensate for the absence or even the breakdown of leadership. When we fail to identify with the idea of leadership embodying prescriptive standards of virtue, character, conscience, of taste and sensibility—and of leaders who elevate us to a higher ground, and who, no less than great visionary poets, make men and women better citizens in their cities—we begin to accept inferior qualities, inferior leaders, inferior aspirations, inferior choices. Joseph Conrad, in his novel *Nostromo* (1904), memorably renders this rhythm of disintegration among leaders who have "but a feeble and imperfect consciousness of the worth and force of the inner life." Particularly in a democracy in which responsibility and freedom must strenuously interact, when the quality of leadership deteriorates there is a comparable deterioration in the actions of the led. It is precisely in the course of this deterioration that we can discern how the demand for and pursuit of leadership are prostituted, that is to say, exposed or subjected to a destructive agency or an impulse devoted to an unworthy or corrupt cause.

The results of this prostitution are all too visible and alarming, as fundamental qualities of leadership are subject more and more to revision, to deconstruction, to use here a word that enjoys much favor in the intellectual community. We reach the point, then, of trivializing the idea, and the ideal, of leadership, and proceed to manufacture multiple substitutes seemingly satisfying the human longing for leadership. That, too, public, and particularly political, leaders not only accommodate but also enact a general loss of standards further weakens the idea of leadership and heightens the atmosphere of cynicism and contempt in the "public square." In a sense, the prostitution of the idea of leadership melds with the pursuit of leadership in non-discriminating ways and forms, opportunity abetted by social scientists and behaviorists, and by commercial and journalistic interests. The sharp decline, too, of the religious idea, even on the part of the religious themselves, adds significantly to the process of prostitution. Ultimately the crumbling of moral climate and spiritual terrain eventuates the crumbling of "the partnership between principle and process...the first fact of life and of our work," to recall one of Lao Tzu's famous sayings.

Any diminution of the moral sense and the discriminating faculty is bound to be pernicious to one's capacity for the recognition, analysis, and measurement of leadership and of its representatives in all areas of human endeavor. And any detrition of standards of leadership must be accompanied by a confluent detrition of the character of leadership and in turn of our estimation of leader-types. Pseudo-leadership and pseudo-leaders characterize current conditions as more and more citizens confuse leadership with the cult of personality and the world of celebrities. Immoral and amoral conditions breed immoral and amoral tendencies. And the leveling or the absence of standards influences one's view of leaders and of the qualities that they project and that, ostensibly, satisfy one's hopes and desires. Our choice of leaders underscores the anomalous and, above all, the antinomian features of American life and character in the modern age. Babbitt is to the point here when he observes: "…we are living in a world that in certain important respects has gone wrong on first principles; which will be found to be another way of saying we are living in a world that has been betrayed by its leaders." Doubtlessly, the scarcity of visionary political and intellectual leadership affects in drastic ways human judgment and selection. Choices are symptomatic of the corrosive tendencies of American civilization and polity as these are impelled by our obsession with change, usually to the detriment of the "permanent things," it need hardly be said. Indeed, what most characterizes the conditions of our situation is a pattern, if not a pathology, of disorder.

This pattern of disorder determines our conceptions of leadership, and of the leaders we choose. Insight, wisdom, authority, faith, and fortitude are neither the virtues nor the values which we necessarily seek or honor in leaders. We make standards subservient to a pluralistic and fragmented society, to Jacobin impulses and doctrines. Those whom we esteem and reward and follow often accede to the disorder-pattern besetting the life of the republic and the life of the soul; such leaders mirror public and private insolvency at the brink of chaos. They project precisely the traits and propensities of those who comprise the "anonymous mass" and who suffer from the malady that Walter Lippmann, in *The Public Philosophy* (1955), pinpoints in these words: "There is a profound disorientation in their experience, a radical disconnection between the notions of their minds and the needs of their souls." Athletes, television stars, and entertainers, Hollywood actors and actresses, smatterers, rock and rap singers and musical groups, publicists, along with pseudo-artists, -academics, and -critics who command enormous attention and acclaim: they encompass the new secularist elite to whom we look for leadership; they set the standards, style, and taste of post-modern, post-managerial society; they become our sentinels of art and letters as they write a new lexicon of thrills and titillation.

What, then, can we say about the prospects of leadership? How can we expect great leadership to emerge from a disjointed culture, "rotten and rotting others"? Can we possibly produce genuine leaders in a society that accommodates or follows "the enemies of the permanent things"? Those who choose to answer these questions buoyantly ignore our present predicament. Nowhere is this predicament better epitomized than in the educational realm in which the canon lies in ruins and arrogant ideologues formulate with an iron fist entire areas of teaching, administration, texts, and policies. "All education today serves to prepare the individual for the world of disjointedness," to recall here Max Picard's observation. In this situation there is neither past nor future; the dogma of presentism thrives everywhere and makes it difficult for any true nourishment or birth of leadership. Hence we must measure realistically and sternly the prospects of leadership against existing realities.

And yet we also cannot be content with an attitude of

"So be it!" or even to practice the despair in virile acceptance some existentialists preach. The possibility of ascent, however perilous it may be, is never extinct, as history has confirmed even in the worst of times and climes. Maintaining, in Eric Voegelin's words, "conscious opposition of the well-ordered soul to the disorder of the society around it" is a major need. Recognizing, too, that political maneuvering is not political leadership is still another major need. Indeed, we have to understand the limits of political leadership itself, neither romanticizing nor exaggerating its possibilities. We can only hope, as T.S. Eliot asserted not long after the end of World War II, that "there will always be situations in which one man, or a few men, will render a service to their society simply by standing alone in an unpopular opinion and telling their countrymen that they are wrong, with no hope of accomplishing anything except witnessing to the truth as they see it."

In a profane age in which paradigms of leadership are not abundant, it is especially important to look first within the inner life of memory and continuity for those values and verities that the outer life has declared inoperative. No tyranny, collective or individual, can outlaw or eradicate the capacity for critical reflection. Of the need to reflect on the qualities and the state of leadership there can be no end. This is doubly true at a time when the subject of leadership seems to be the exclusive property of clever journalists, television celebrities, best-selling authors, political pundits, and pollsters who glibly spell out the function and constituents of leadership, with very little regard for its moral dimension and responsibilities.

It is worth noting that the twentieth century has variously excited significant reflections on the phenomenon of violence. For instance, *Reflections on Violence* (1908), by the French social theorist and "metaphysician of socialism," Georges Sorel, argues the case for an "ethics of violence" and praises the role of violence as an agent of progress and amelioration. And from an opposing vantage point there is the celebrated essay entitled "*The Iliad, Poem of Might,*" by the Christian Hellenist metaphysician of "the invisible Church," Simone Weil, who sees violence as an example of demonic might that "makes a thing of man, for it makes him a corpse." Such reflections on violence should definitely claim our consideration if we are to locate and resist its principalities and powers. But no less legitimate and no less necessary, we also have to reflect on the nature of leadership, and of leadership that can help us soar beyond the walls of violence within which life is often trapped. Surely the nexus between violence and leadership can hardly be escaped.

We need to restore moral value to leadership, and thus free it not only from its purely sociological and political contexts, but also from its empirical configurations. Leadership is yet another word that has been emptied of its hierarchical order and has experienced the same dismal fate of other words of absolute value—loyalty, nobility, virtue, goodness, generosity, honor. No less than these words, leadership relates to the struggle between good and evil. We need to save the meaning of leadership from the kind of devaluation that tears down the structure of language and, in effect, the structure of truth. Robbed of its moral value and detached from universal referents and specificity of standards, leadership is stripped of its dignity. The whole question of leadership, as Babbitt emphasizes, is primarily moral; indeed, the true leader is ultimately "the man who is so loyal to sound standards that he inspires right conduct in others by the sheer rightness of his example." When the idea of leadership falls into the realm of the vacuous, it honors no moral imperative and is absorbed by degraded conditions and oblique purposes. As a result we make leadership an equivocal commodity— purchasable, temporalized, manipulated, condemned to unending alteration. The moral measure of leadership, in these circumstances, is supplanted by *ersatz* forms and types ordained by the ruling spirit of the time.

In the order of human existence in society and history the problem of leadership is, and has always been, one that involves human destiny. More than at any time in history, and especially now as we are about to enter a new century, we have every reason to heed Edmund Burke's warning: "We must have leaders. If none will undertake to lead us right, we shall find guides who will contrive to conduct us to shame and ruin."

# Appendix

## Irving Babbitt,
## A Chronicle of His Life and Work, 1865-1933*

**1865**  Irving Babbitt is born in Dayton, Ohio, on August 2, the third son and fourth child of the five children of Edwin Dwight and Augusta (Darling) Babbitt.

He comes of a family founded in America by Edward Bobet, or Bobbett (later spelled Babbitt), an Englishman who settled in Plymouth, Massachusetts, in 1643. The Earl of Shaftesbury is reputed to be in the family line.

At the time of Irving's birth, Dr. Babbitt, a physician, is a partner, with Abram Wilt, in a business/commercial school founded in Dayton.

Irving later takes a certain pride in his midwestern origins, feeling there might be a "more robust though unfortunately less combative humanism in the Middle West than on the Atlantic seaboard."

———————————

*This chronicle is an expanded version of *"Irving Babbitt: A Chronology of His Life and Major Works, 1865-1933"* in *Irving Babbitt in Our Time* (1986), edited by George A. Panichas and Claes G. Ryn. The excerpts quoted here are drawn from *Irving Babbitt: Man and Teacher*, edited by Frederick Manchester and Odell Shepard. Published in 1941, this composite biography pays tribute to his power and influence as a teacher. It contains thirty-nine independent memoirs by Babbitt's students, colleagues, and friends. Arranged in chronological order, the biographical narrative is presented from many points of view.

Also worthy of mention here is *"Irving Babbitt and the Teaching of Literature,"* a pamphlet of twenty-eight pages, containing the inaugural lecture given at Harvard University, November 7, 1960, by Harry Levin, the first to hold the Irving Babbitt Professorship of Comparative Literature. This lecture is an eloquent account of Babbitt as man and teacher and critic.

The family moves frequently during his childhood, even as far east as New York City and East Orange, New Jersey, where Irving attends public schools.

He sells newspapers on the New York City streets, where he plays with and frequently gives black eyes and bloody noses to street urchins.

**1876** Irving's mother dies when he is about eleven years old. Her parents take Irving, one of his older brothers, Tom, and his younger sister, Katharine, to live with them on the Darling farm in Madisonville, Ohio, on the outskirts of Cincinnati.

In Madisonville Irving attends a small district school. He often helps tenant farmers pick fruit and vegetables in the nearby fields and woods.

**1881** Dr. Edwin Babbitt has remarried and is living in Cincinnati. Irving and his sister Katharine live at their father's home and attend Woodward High School, where other students are impressed with his knowledge and reading. He graduates second in a class of approximately fifty without seeming to work for grades or to care about them.

A classmate describes him as "affable, always agreeable, a likable boy among boys; never forward or domineering, but not a shrinking violet either."

At the age of sixteen he receives a high pass in an examination that qualifies him to teach in a district school.

Irving's brother Tom is now a foreman on his uncle Albert Babbitt's Bar-Circle Ranch in Cheyenne, Wyoming. When Irving spends a summer there, sometimes riding horseback for fourteen hours a day, he develops a strenuous robustness and an almost Homeric love of nature.

These traits surface throughout his adult life, especially in strenuous tennis and jogging, in "super-pedestrianism":

"In Paris, at the midnight hour, the police around the Luxembourg Gardens mistook for a robber pursued by his victim what proved to be Babbitt and his gymnastic convert, the Norwegian mathematician Palmbad, circling the park at full speed."

**1882** Unable to attend college because of a lack of funds, Irving returns to high school to study chemistry and civil engineering. His chief family tie, at this time, seems to be his sister Katharine. Throughout his life he remains deeply attached to her.

**1885** With financial help from his uncles—Thomas Babbitt of Dayton and Albert Babbitt of Cheyenne—Irving moves east to attend Harvard University.

He travels to Cambridge, Massachusetts, alone, knowing no one there, and rooms at College House.

As an undergraduate he studies languages, including French, German, Italian, Spanish, Greek, and Latin.

**1887** In the summer Irving and a classmate, A. P. Butterworth, sail to Europe. They stay five days in Paris, then walk to Madrid, Italy, Switzerland, and down the Rhine to Holland. They travel from Havre to Gibraltar, from Naples to the North Sea.

Butterworth recalls their living as tramps, with knapsacks on their backs, "sleeping in the fields, or in the small inns, shunning the beaten paths, not intent on the sights, mingling with the common people, walking the highways with them, drinking in their talk in the inns or in their homes and their farms."

In 1898, Babbitt's *Atlantic Monthly* essay on "Lights and Shades of Spanish Character" is graced by charming, even lyrical memories of this "European jaunt."

**1889** Irving graduates with high honors from the Department of Classics at Harvard.

In September he takes the first job offered to him by a teachers' agency. He leaves for Montana, to teach Greek and Latin at the College of Montana, in Deer Lodge.

The two years he spends at this small Presbyterian school are to be the last time he teaches classical languages.

**1891** He goes to Paris to study Sanskrit and Pāli, along with Indian philosophy, under the direction of Sylvain Lévi, a Hindu scholar, only two years older than Irving, at the *Ecole des Hautes Etudes*.

**1892** Returning to Harvard University to study for the M.A., Babbitt meets Paul Elmer More. He and Irving are the only two students in Professor Charles Rockwell Lanman's advanced class in Oriental studies.

"I can well remember our first meeting," More reminisces, "in Lanman's marvellously equipped library. Babbitt was rather above the average height, powerfully built, with the complexion of radiant health.... But it was his eyes that caught and held one's attention. They were of a dark, not pure blue, and even then, though of a luster that dimmed somewhat in later years, had in repose the withdrawn look of one much given to meditation."

**1893** Babbitt is awarded an M.A. by Harvard Graduate School.

In the autumn he is appointed for a one-year instructorship in Romance languages at Williams College, taking the place of Professor Morton, who is on a leave of absence.

He teaches French, Spanish, and Italian, as well as a course on Dante for juniors and seniors.

**1894** He returns to Harvard to join the Department of Classics.

Since 1883, when President Charles W. Eliot dropped the classical language requirements from the curriculum, Harvard's Department of Classics has been dwindling. Chairman William Goodwin finds he has no position to offer Babbitt.

He teaches Romance languages, as an instructor of French, from 1894-1902.

"I may be pardoned," Paul Elmer More reflects, "for adding here my complaint that a very great teacher, perhaps even the greatest this country has ever produced, was overlooked by one department and , where accepted, had to force his way up against resistance and through protracted depreciation."

**1895** He delivers, at the University of Wisconsin, a lecture on "The Rational Study of the Classics."

The lecture's subsequent publication in March 1897, in *The Atlantic Monthly,* marks Babbitt's first appearance in print.

**1896** Probably through the intervention of President Eliot, Babbitt is relieved of teaching elementary French in the first semester of 1896-1897.

He teaches advanced "half-courses" for upperclassmen and graduate students.

Babbitt's relationship to President Eliot, although most advantageous to his career, at this point, in that Babbitt could receive a sympathetic audience from Eliot for his point of view, is steeped in ambiguity, especially with respect to Babbitt's attitude toward the Elective System in effect at Harvard.

He begins teaching additional courses at Radcliffe College.

He visits France in the summer and purchases about 300 books in further preparation for teaching more advanced French courses.

**1897** The French neoclassical and conservative literary critic Vincent de Paul Marie Ferdinand Brunetière's (1849-1906) visits Harvard. Babbitt is one of his hosts.

Babbitt subsequently translates Brunetière's *"The French Mastery of Style"* and publishes the translation in *The Atlantic Monthly* in October.

His sister Katharine is a frequent visitor. Meeting her with Babbitt at Harvard a graduate student remarks: "Babbitt's dear attachment to his sister Katharine—so distinguished intellectually, so refined in her tastes, so sure in her judgments —was touching."

**1898** He edits, with an essay on Hippolyte Adolphe Taine (1828-1893), Taine's *Introduction à l'Histoire de la Littérature Anglaise.*

**1900** Babbitt marries, in London, his former Radcliffe student, Dora May Drew. Born and brought up in China Mrs. Babbitt is the twenty-three-year-old daughter of Edward B. Drew, a Protestant missionary to China whose home is in Cambridge, Massachusetts.

The Babbitts rent a three-story house at 6 Kirkland Road, in Cambridge, on the third floor of which Irving has a private study. Among their neighbors are Josiah Royce, William James, and Charles Rockwell Lanman.

"The house, which was in a quiet neighborhood, bore witness to the taste and culture of its occupants. Turkish rugs covered the floors, the walls were pleasantly tinted, and in the living room...the center of interest was a red brick fireplace with a white mantel. Near the door of the living room was a small set of bookshelves, on the top of which stood several volumes of Boswell's *Life of Johnson*."

"There were few pictures...[among them] the calm and lovely face of Henner's *'Fabiola'* and Guido Reni's *'St. Michael and the Dragon.'* On the table beside the fireplace stood a large reading lamp, beneath which lay often a copy of *The Atlantic Monthly,* to which Babbitt was contributing. The lampshade had a Chinese dragon on it, and some of the other fabrics in the room bore Chinese designs."

**1901** The Babbitt's daughter, Esther, is born on October 2.

**1902** Babbitt is promoted to assistant professor. He edits, with an Introduction and notes, Renan's *Souvenirs d'Enfance et de Jeunesse.*

**1903** The Babbitt's son, Edward Sturges, is born on June 12.

**1905** Babbitt edits, with an Introduction, notes, and vocabulary, Voltaire's *Zadig and Other Stories.*

**1907** He is awarded a sabbatical leave to finish his first book.

He spends part of his sabbatical in Paris and part visiting England, where he walks in the Lake Country.

**1908** Babbitt's first book, *Literature and the American College*, is published.

He visits France, where many of his friends from his student days are now professors at the Sorbonne.

Abbott Lawrence Lowell becomes president of Harvard.

**1909** Student interest in Babbitt's classes swells. T.S. Eliot enrolls in his course on "Literary Criticism in France with Special Reference to the Nineteenth Century."

He publishes "On Being Original" in *The Atlantic Monthly*.

**1910** Babbitt's second book, *The New Laokoon: An Essay on the Confusion of the Arts,* is published.

He edits, with an Introduction and notes, Racine's *Phèdre*.

Now teaching larger advanced courses, he complains to Paul Elmer More about Harvard's failure to recognize him.

He becomes increasingly disenchanted with President Lowell and begins to look elsewhere for a teaching position.

**1912** Only after he has been offered a professorship at the University of Illinois is Babbitt promoted to professor of French literature.

His teaching continues to be mainly in the area of comparative literature, however.

Babbitt's third book, *The Masters of Modern French Literature,* is published.

**1915** He spends part of a "semi-sabbatical" in Dublin, New Hampshire, working on *Rousseau and Romanticism*.

In October, he proofreads the ninth series of Paul Elmer More's *Shelburne Essays*. He and More continue to exchange manuscripts for criticism and proofreading.

**1918** By the end of World War I, Babbitt is widely recognized as "a great man." He is distinguished in appearance, powerful in physique, with patrician features set off by fine gray hair.

In Paris, students at the Sorbonne view him as a continental gentleman, a Socratic influence, a modern sage.

**1919** His fourth book, *Rousseau and Romanticism*, is published.

In the summer he begins work on a book he intends to call *Democracy and Imperialism*, published in 1924 as *Democracy and Leadership*.

**1920** He is Larwill lecturer at Kenyon College in January, speaking to graduate students in the Crufts Physics Laboratory, "of all places," on "The Discipline of Ideas in Literature," published in the *English Journal* in February as "English and the Discipline of Ideas."

Arthur Lovejoy reviews *Rousseau and Romanticism* in *Modern Language Notes* and charges Babbitt with being "romantic" in his very anti-romanticism. Babbitt is provoked to one of his few responses to criticism: "In ingenuous and complicated misapprehension of my point of view he has easily outdone all my other reviewers."

**1921** From October 1921 to February 1922, Babbitt is Harvard lecturer at Yale.

**1922** He is West lecturer at Stanford University in April.

**1923** From March to May, Babbitt is James Hazen Hyde Lecturer and exchange professor at the Sorbonne.

He gives two courses—one in French on Rousseau and one in English on the English Romantic poets.

Irving, his wife, and his sister, Katharine, spend several months at the *Hôtel des Saints-Pères* in Paris.

His reputation in France exceeds even his reputation in America; the lectures are a triumphant success; he is hailed as the "the man of the hour." Babbitt is often surrounded by Oriental students, not only Chinese, but also Japanese, Korean, and Hindu.

**1924** His fifth book, *Democracy and Leadership*, is published.

**1925** In November Katharine Babbitt is killed in an automobile accident.

"I was well enough acquainted with her," Paul Elmer More writes in a letter to Babbitt, "to know how loyal and helpful a sister she had been, and how utterly unselfish she was. To me she can be a beautiful memory, but I understand what her loss is to you."

**1926** Paul Elmer More substitutes at Harvard for Professor Charles Burton Gulick in the Department of Classics during the second term of the academic year of 1925-1926. He meets with Babbitt two or three times a week to discuss the tenets of neo-humanism.

Babbitt gives an address in October on "Humanist and Specialist" at the dedication of the Marston Hall of Languages at Brown University in Providence, Rhode Island.

He becomes a corresponding member of the French Institute *(Académie des Sciences Morales et Politiques)*.

**1927** Babbitt's lifelong interest in Oriental philosophy and religion and the relations between East and West is crystallized in "Buddha and the Occident," which he now begins writing.

"Buddha and the Occident," his spiritual testament, later serves as the Introduction to his translation of the ancient Pāli classic of Buddhist wisdom, *The Dhammapada* (published posthumously in 1936).

Selections from this essay subsequently appear as "Romanticism and the Orient" (in the *Bookman* in 1931) and in *On Being Creative and Other Essays* (1932).

**1928** Babbitt publishes in *The Forum* in February one of his most comprehensive essays, "The Critic and American Life," in which he attacks H.L. Mencken and anti-traditionalism.

He goes to Italy, Greece, France, and England on a pleasure trip.

**1929** Babbitt restates his views on "President Eliot and American Education" in *The Forum* (January 1929).

**1930** He is Clyde Fitch lecturer at Amherst College.

He is elected to the American Academy of Arts and Letters.

On May 9, he debates Carl Van Doren and Henry Seidel Canby in Carnegie Hall.

Van Doren and Canby are favored by the audience; the loudspeaker system breaks down. "Though it was a very warm day," Babbitt says upon returning to Cambridge, "the occasion might be described as a frost."

Controversy rages over Babbitt's and More's neohumanism. Babbitt publishes an important chapter, "Humanism: An Essay at Definition," in *Humanism and America*, edited by Norman Foerster.

**1931** Babbitt delivers the Alexander lectures in Toronto, his last important lecture series.

**1932** His health begins to decline in January.

He delivers the commencement address at Drew Seminary

in Madison, New Jersey, in May.

He is awarded an honorary Doctor of Humane Letters degree from Bowdoin College in June.

On November 12, he delivers before the American Academy of Arts and Letters his last public lecture, "Style in a Democracy," published in *Spanish Character and Other Essays* (1940) as "The Problem of Style in a Democracy."

He sees T.S. Eliot twice in November.

He publishes his sixth book, *On Being Creative and Other Essays*.

**1933** In much pain as his health deteriorates, Babbitt fulfills all his academic responsibilities through the final examinations at Harvard.

He dies at his home in Cambridge on July 15.

"On an afternoon of July," the Bowdoin College professor G.R. Elliott writes, "his body lay silent in the chancel of the new Harvard chapel. That final scene was strange, hard to believe; though all of its externals were congruous enough. The service was austerely plain. Passages of excellent moral scripture, Christian and non-Christian, were recited from the high reading-desk, which closed a vista of white walls made whiter by the light of day. But the casket, beneath the desk, was covered with a crimson pall; and the sentences that were uttered above it had in them frequent words of rich and deep color. There came to me and doubtless to others who were present a mysterious, overmastering sense of a glow of life in white light...."

Following his funeral, Louis J. A. Mercier recalls, "we were soon scattered and I walked toward Widener, where I had so often met with him. Then I turned back. The squirrels were still gamboling and the pigeons pecking on the green. The shadows of the elms still played on the walls. The golden light still suffused the scene. But not a single human being was now in sight. I just caught a glimpse of a high black car disappearing down the sunlit path. Irving Babbitt was crossing a gate of the Harvard Yard for the last time. The bell was tolling...."

# Notes

## Chapter I

1. "Humanizing Society," in *The Critique of Humanism: A Symposium,* ed. C. Hartley Grattan (New York, 1930), 68, 84.

2. "Humanism and Naturalism," *Reactionary Essays on Poetry and Ideas* (New York, 1936), 114. This essay first appeared under the title "The Fallacy of Humanism," *Criterion,* Vol. 8 (1929), 661-81, and then in *The Critique of Humanism: A Symposium,* 131-66.

3. *Criticism: The Major Texts,* ed. Walter Jackson Bate (New York, 1952), 547.

4. *American Renaissance: Art and Expression in the Age of Emerson and Whitman* (London and New York, 1941), 231.

5. *Shelburne Essays,* 7th ser. (New York, 1910), 219, 220.

6. *Irving Babbitt: Man and Teacher,* ed. Frederick Manchester and Odell Shepard (New York, 1941), 104.

7. *Ibid.,* 90.

8. "Irving Babbitt, Paul More, and Transcendentalism," in *Transcendentalism and Its Legacy,* ed. Myron Simon and Thornton H. Parsons (Ann Arbor, 1966), 191.

9. "The Cry in the Wilderness," *Aspects of Literature* (New York, 1920), 170.

10. *The Lion and the Honeycomb: Essays in Solicitude and Critique* (New York, 1955), 147.

11. "The Humanism of Irving Babbitt," *Selected Essays* (New York, 1960), 421.

12. "Irving Babbitt," *On Being Human, New Shelburne Essays,* 3rd ser. (Princeton, 1936), 29.

13. *Ibid.,* 42. This essay first appeared in the *University of Toronto Quarterly,* Vol. 3 (1934), 129-45; it was later reprinted in *Irving Babbitt: Man and Teacher,* 322-37.

## Chapter II

1. *Criticism: The Major Texts*, 547.

2. *Letters on Literature and Politics*, 1912-1972, ed. Elena Wilson (New York, 1977), 195.

3. "Lights and Shades of Spanish Character," *Spanish Character and Other Essays*, ed. Frederick Manchester, Rachel Giese, William F. Giese (Boston and New York, 1940).

4. "A Revival of Humanism," *The Bookman* (March 1930), 7, 9.

## Chapter III

1. Quoted in *Irving Babbitt: Man and Teacher*, 229.

2. New York, 1942, 300.

3. "Irving Babbitt," *On Being Human*, 37.

4. *New England Saints* (Ann Arbor, 1956), v.

5. *American Renaissance*, 231.

6. "Introduction: Holiness in History and Holiness Today," in Roland Cluny, *Holiness in Action* (New York, 1963), 10.

7. *New England Saints*, 149, 152.

8. See review of George A. Panichas, *The Courage of Judgment: Essays in Criticism, Culture, and Society* (Knoxville, 1982), in *Christianity and Literature* (Winter 1983), 83.

9. These essays are included in *Selected Essays*, 419-38.

10. *The Heretics* (New York, 1962), 10.

11. "Is Humanism a Religion?" *The Bookman* (May 1929), 241.

12. "A Revival of Humanism," *The Bookman* (March 1930), 9.

13. *New England Saints*, 159-60.

14. *On Being Human*, 37.

15. *The Nation* (October 18, 1917), 428.

16. "Humanism and Symbolic Imagination: Notes on Re-Reading Irving Babbitt," *The Lion and the Honeycomb*, 153.

17. *Metaphysics*, 1072.[b]

## Chapter V

1. With a new Introduction by Claes G. Ryn and an index to all of Babbitt's books (New Brunswick and London, 1995 [1940]).

2. With a Foreword by Russell Kirk and a Preface by Ted J. Smith III (Bryn Mawr, 1995 [1964]).

## Chapter VI

1. *Essays of Four Decades* (Chicago, 1968), 13.

2. Quoted in E. R. Curtius's essay on "The Fundamental Features of Goethe's World," *Essays on European Literature* (Princeton, 1973), 82.

3. See Claes G. Ryn, "*Non Videri Sed Esse*: Folke Leander (1910-1981)," *Modern Age: A Quarterly Review* (Winter 1983), 56-60.

4. "Francis Herbert Bradley," *Selected Essays*, 399.

5. See "Literary Criticism and Philosophy," *The Common Pursuit* (London, 1952), 211-22.

6. *Irving Babbitt: Representative Writings*, ed. George A. Panichas (Lincoln, Neb., 1981), 64-65.

7. *The Responsibilities of the Critic: Essays and Reviews by F. O. Matthiessen*, selected by John Rackliffe (New York, 1952), 165.

8. "A New England Group and Others," *Shelburne Essays*, 11th ser. (New York, 1967 [1921]), 94.

9. *On Being Creative and Other Essays* (Boston, 1932), 204.

## Chapter VII

1. "Conservatives as a Creative Minority," *Modern Age* (Winter 1998), 14.

2. With a Foreword by Russell Kirk (Indianapolis, 1979).

# A Bibliographical Note

"Teacher and Critic" was first published as the Introduction to my *Irving Babbitt: Representative Writings* (Lincoln: University of Nebraska Press, 1981), vii-xxxix.

"The Critical Mission" first appeared as Chapter 2, "The Critical Mission of Irving Babbitt," in my *The Courage of Judgment: Essays in Criticism, Culture, and Society,* with a Foreword by Austin Warren (Knoxville: University of Tennessee Press, 1982), 54-84.

"Babbitt and Religion" was first published in *Modern Age: A Quarterly Review* (Spring/Summer 1984), 169-180, and subsequently in *Irving Babbitt in Our Time,* edited by George A. Panichas and Claes G. Ryn (Washington, D.C.: Catholic University of America Press, 1986), 27-49.

"Irving Babbitt and Simone Weil" was first published in *Comparative Literature Studies* (June 1978), 177-192, and then as Chapter 3 of my *The Critic as Conservator: Essays in Literature, Society, and Culture* (Washington, D.C.: Catholic University of America Press, 1992), 36-53.

"Irving Babbitt and Richard Weaver" first appeared in *Modern Age* (Summer 1996), 267-276.

Part I of "The Widening of the Circle" first appeared as "Irving Babbitt and the Widening of the Circle" in *Modern Age* (Spring 1987), 164-171; Part II was first published in the same journal (Summer 1997) as "Character and Criticism," 287-290.

Parts I-III of "An Act of Reparation" first appeared in *Modern Age* (Summer 1980), 296-303; Part IV was first published in the same journal (Fall 1996) as "Reflections on Leadership," 307-311.

The essays cited above have been reworked for inclusion in this book. Changes vary from essay to essay, and when and where these have been made it has been mainly for the purpose of transition and flow. In integrating and ordering the individual essays I have adhered to a thematic rather than a chronological approach, and one that seeks for structural unity. In terms of the revisions, interconnections, and sequence of the essays, my guiding principle has been that of capturing the special values of my appreciation of Babbitt's total achievement.

Through the years, as my essays have appeared in print, and especially my anthology entitled *Irving Babbitt: Representative Writings,* happily still in print, a number of my readers have prodded me to make available a full-length study of Babbitt's work and thought. It remained for Jeffrey O. Nelson, Vice President for Publications, of the Intercollegiate Studies Institute, Inc., to give me the final nudge. Here I want to record my debt to Mr. Nelson for all his encouragement that now culminates in the publication of *The Critical Legacy of Irving Babbitt: An Appreciation.*

I am pleased to be able to conclude this book with an appendix that features a chronicle of Irving Babbitt's life and work. This chronicle has been carefully and copiously prepared by my long-time research assistant, Mary E. Slayton, who has also made the index. Without her constant assistance this book could not have been published.

# Index

# Index

Derrida, Jacques: and Michel Foucault, 161; a "prophet of extremity," 161

Depression, the Great. *See* Great Depression, the

De Sales, Saint Francis. *See* Francis de Sales, Saint

De Staël, Madame. *See* Staël, Madame de

Dewey, John, 184; influence of, 9-10, 114, 141; and the "inner check," 172; and man's moral nature, 152; radical optimism of, 9-10, 171-72; Eliseo Vivas on, 184

*Dhammapada, The,* 78, 165, 203; and Irving Babbitt's religious ethos, 95

Disorder: as anarchy, 133; and leadership, 189; in the form of nominalism, 132; and order, 132, 191; as romanticism, 131-32; and Jean Jacques Rousseau, 94, 131-32, 139; spiritual, 94; and William of Ockham, 132; and World War I, 131; and World War II, 132. *See also* Order

Dostoevsky, Fyodor M.: *Crime and Punishment,* 107

Drew, Dora May. *See* Babbitt, Dora May

Drew, Edward B. (father-in-law), 199

Drew Seminary, 204-205

Dualism, 24; between two wills, 17-18; of Buddha, 96; and evil, 37, 51; and the "higher will," 18; and humanism, 94; and Paul Elmer More, 173; "new dualism," 50-51, 134; "older dualism," 51, 173; and the principle of control, 18; of Jean Jacques Rousseau, 50-51; social dualism, 51; and the "will to refrain," 17-18

Duties: and rights, 73, 126

Earnest, Ernest: critical of Irving Babbitt, 176

Eckermann, Johann Peter: *Conversations with Goethe,* 94

*Ecole des Hautes Etudes,* 197

Education: American, 39, 136-37; Irving Babbitt's and Richard M. Weaver's differing views on, 136-42; of character, 135, 138; and John Dewey, 141; Elective System of, 39, 137, 198; and Charles W. Eliot, 39, 137, 198; Ralph Waldo Emerson's "true scholar," 67; German scholasticism, 39, 56; Gnostics of, 135-36, 139-40; and humanism, 57-58 (*humanitas,* 58); and ideology, 138-39, 190; Russell Kirk on, 136; and literary studies, 1, 59, 135, 164; Max Picard on, 190; of the soul, 139; specialization

29, 35; Rousseauistic illusion, 118; and self-restraint, 21

Imagination, 34; Arcadian, 35; Aristotle on, 31, 61; and Matthew Arnold, 150; artistic, 68; Edmund Burke on, 30, 115; creative, 31, 125; Benedetto Croce on, 157; ethical, 30 (and art), 35-36, 61, 143; idyllic, 157, 158, 180; and illusion, 33; moral, 27, 125, 157-58, 180; and reason, 149-63; and reverie, 29; romantic, 29; Rousseauistic, 30, 115, 157, 180; of the Spanish character, 75; undisciplined, 53; Simone Weil on, 125-26; and will, 149-63

Individualism: Edmund Burke on, 30; naturalistic, 30; and personality, 32; and rights and duties, 73; Jean Jacques Rousseau on, 30; and Simone Weil, 113

Inner check, 166; and aestheticism, 27-28; and American culture, 175; of Buddha, 96; and John Dewey, 172; *vs.* eleutheromania, 153; T.S. Eliot on, 88; and the "higher will," 9, 18, 156, 157; and humanism, 9; "inner control," 60; and the law of control, 96; of the man of character, 182; Paul Elmer More on, 153; and religion, 9; and Jean Jacques Rousseau, 188, 165; applied to temperamental impulse, 96. *See also Elan vital; Frein vital;* Will

Institute of France; 8

"Interpreting India to the West" (Irving Babbitt): and Buddhism, 95-96; on "spiritual athletes" and "cosmic loafers," 132-33

*Introduction à l'Histoire de la Littérature Anglaise* (Hippolyte Taine), 199

Intuition: and the One and the Many, 30, 92; two orders of, 68

*Irving Babbitt* (Stephen C. Brennan and Stephen R. Yarbrough), 165

*Irving Babbitt: An Intellectual Study* (Thomas R. Nevin), 165

"Irving Babbitt and the Teaching of Literature" (Harry Levin), 194

*Irving Babbitt in Our Time* (George A. Panichas and Claes G. Ryn, editors), 194

*Irving Babbitt, Literature and the Democratic Culture* (Milton Hindus): analyzed, 163-69

*Irving Babbitt: Man and Teacher* (Frederick Manchester and Odell Shepard, editors), 194

"Island, The" (George Gordon, Lord Byron), 27

"Is There a Marxist Doctrine?" (Simone Weil), 118

Jacobins: Edmund Burke's response to, 41

# Index

Mencken, H. L.: criticism by Babbitt, 204; on New Humanism, 9; and anti-traditionalism, 204

Mercier, Louis J.A.: on Irving Babbitt, 91, 205

*Metaphysics* (Aristotle), 106

Minerva (goddess): compared to Irving Babbitt, 40

*Modern Language Notes,* 202

Modernism: and asceticism, 26; modern literature, 61-63; modern movement (failure of), 82; and Jean Jacques Rousseau, 50-51, 94, 131-32, 165; and standards, 66-67, 110, 185

Montgomery, Marion: on Irving Babbitt's humanism, 87

Morality: Irving Babbitt as a moralist, 55, 67, 150; and beauty, 68, 127; and John Dewey, 152; ethical-moral standards, 15, 22, 55, 60-61, 149, 156-57; and imagination, 27, 30, 125, 157-58, 180; moral criticism, 28, 142-43; moral fascism, 10, 88; moral function of art, 157; "New Morality of drifting," 19; and *The Rime of the Ancient Mariner,* 31; romantic morality, 27; and violence, 192

More, Paul Elmer, 41; his criticism of Irving Babbitt, 69; on Irving Babbitt's criticism, 40, 123; his

friendship with Irving Babbitt, 7, 8, 197; on Irving Babbitt's lack of recognition, 39, 198, 201; on Irving Babbitt's lack of religion, 81-82, 84, 85, 92, 173; on Buddhism, 99 (on Irving Babbitt's Buddhism, 95); on the dogma of grace, 81; and T.S. Eliot, 81, 88; on Ralph Waldo Emerson, 161-62; on humanism, 81; on the "inner check," 153; on *Literature and the American College,* 57; New Humanism of, 8, 146-47, 203, 204; on the "New Morality of drifting," 19; criticized by *The New Republic,* 11; on "The Rational Study of the Classics," 56-57; on Roman Catholicism, 81; on Allen Tate; and the *Upanishads,* 99; Rebecca West on, 11
—*The Catholic Faith,* 81, 99
—*Christ the Word,* 81
—"Criticism," 11
—*New Shelburne Essays,* 173
—"On Being Human," 173
—*Shelburne Essays,* 201

Morton, Professor, 197

Murry, John Middleton: on *Rousseau and Romanticism,* 20

Mysticism: and asceticism, 51, 90; and Christianity, 81; T.S. Eliot on, 101; Hindu, 99; pyschological, 101; of Simone Weil, 111, 123

Napoleon Bonaparte, 136, 180;

# Index

# Index

*Babbitt,* 165

Yeats, William Butler, 28; heresy
  of, 87

*Zadig and Other Stories* (Voltaire),
  200

Ziegler, Leopold: on heresy, 89